"This book is a game changer for researchers drawing on postqualitative educational research in postdigital times. The authors have produced an exceptional storying of methodology and theory that opens thinking and practice. The text offers practical definitions and ways of working found in the writings of known and new thinkers. The book's greatest achievement is the decentering of Western ways of knowing from the study of global children. A highlight is to read about children from the global south as children, not as deficit children or deficit Adults."

Professor Annette Woods, *School of Early Childhood and Inclusive Education. Queensland University of Technology*

"Staying with the discomfort produced by having to conform to the requirements of a large-scale international research project, these researchers from the global south re-turn to the data they collected. They show how data reveals itself differently in relation to posthuman, postdigital, and decolonial theories. Concepts and methods relating to the *Posts-* are clearly explained and put to work, unsettling taken-for-granted assumptions about developmentalism, play, and qualitative research methods. This opens the way for re-imaginings of research subjects, transcription, research sites, and data analysis, in other words, for doing research differently. This accessible account is a must for scholars interested in under-taking postqualitative research."

Professor Hilary Janks, *Professor Emerita University of the Witwatersrand, South Africa*

POSTDIGITAL PLAY AND GLOBAL EDUCATION

Postdigital Play and Global Education: Reconfiguring Research is a re-turn to a large-scale, international project on children's digital play. Adopting postqualitative and posthumanist theories, research practices are reconfigured all the way down from what counts as 'data', 'tools', 'instruments', 'transcription', research sites', 'researchers', to notions of responsibility and accountability in qualitative research. Through a series of vignettes involving complex human and more-than-human collaborators (e.g., GoPros, octopus, avatars, diaries, sackball, LEGO bricks), the authors challenge who and what can be playful and creative across contexts in the global north and global south. The diffractive methodology enacted interrupts Western developmental notions of agency that are dominant in research involving young children.

The concept of 'postdigital' offers fresh opportunities to disrupt dominant understandings of children's play. Play emerges as an enigmatic and shape-shifting human and more-than-human agentic force that operates beyond digital/non-digital, online/offline binaries. By attuning to race, gender, age and language, invisible and colonising aspects of postdigital worldings the authors show how global education research can be reimagined through a posthumanist decentering of children without erasure.

Postdigital Play and Global Education puts into practice Karen Barad's agential realism, but also a range of postdevelopmental and posthumanist writings from diverse fields. The book will be of particular interest to researchers looking for guidance to enact agential realist and posthumanist philosophies in research involving young children.

Kerryn Dixon is Associate Professor at the University of Nottingham, UK. Her teaching and research are in the field of language and literacy studies, specialising in early literacy and critical literacy. She is particularly interested in the interrelationships between language, literacy, and power in contexts of poverty.

Karin Murris is Professor of Early Childhood Education at the University of Oulu, Finland, and Emerita Professor of Pedagogy and Philosophy, University of Cape Town, South Africa. She is a teacher educator, grounded in academic philosophy and a postqualitative research paradigm. Her main interests are in posthuman child studies, philosophy in education, ethics, and democratic pedagogies. Website: www.karinmurris.com.

Joanne Peers is a PhD candidate at The University of Oulu, Finland, pursuing relationality in environmental education through thinking with bodies and water. Her interest in justice in the global south is woven through her role as Head of Academics at The Centre for Creative Education in Cape Town.

Theresa Giorza is a researcher and teacher in Childhood Studies with an interest in arts-based pedagogies and philosophical enquiry. She is based at the Centre for Creative Education in Cape Town. Her book, *Learning with Damaged Colonial Places: Posthumanist Pedagogies from a Joburg Preschool* was published in 2021 by Springer.

Chanique Lawrence is an experienced Linguist, who has worked as a professional translator and transcriber. As a Linguist her work is focussed on representing global south communities. Currently based in the Netherlands, Chanique is pursuing her Master's at Leiden University where she is focusing on Human Rights Law.

Postqualitative, New Materialist and Critical Posthumanist Research

Editor in Chief:

Karin Murris
Universities of Oulu, Finland, and Cape Town, South Africa

Editors:

Vivienne Bozalek, *University of the Western Cape and Rhodes University, South Africa*
Asilia Franklin-Phipps, *State University of New York at New Paltz, USA*
Simone Fullagar, *Griffith University, Australia*
Candace R. Kuby, *University of Missouri, USA*
Karen Malone, *Swinburne University of Technology, Australia*
Carol A. Taylor, *University of Bath, United Kingdom*
Weili Zhao, *Hangzhou Normal University, China*

This cutting-edge series is designed to assist established researchers, academics, postgraduate/graduate students, and their supervisors across higher education faculties and departments to incorporate novel, postqualitative, new materialist, and critical posthumanist approaches in their research projects and their academic writing. In addition to these substantive foci, books within the series are inter-, multi-, or transdisciplinary and are in dialogue with perspectives such as Black feminisms and Indigenous knowledges, decolonial, African, Eastern, and young children's philosophies. Although the series' primary aim is accessibility, its scope makes it attractive to established academics already working with postqualitative approaches.

This series is unique in providing short, user-friendly, affordable books that support postgraduate students and academics across disciplines and faculties in higher education. The series is supported by its own website with videos, images, and other forms of 3D transmodal expression of ideas—provocations for research courses.

More resources for the books in the series are available on the series website, www .postqualitativeresearch.com.

If you are interested in submitting a proposal for the series, please write to the Chief Editor, Professor Karin Murris: karin.murris@oulu.fi; karin.murris@uct.ac.za.

Other volumes in this series include:

For a full list of titles in this series, please visit: www.routledge.com/Postqualitative -New-Materialist-and-Critical-Posthumanist-Research/book-series/PNMR

POSTDIGITAL PLAY AND GLOBAL EDUCATION

Reconfiguring Research

*Kerryn Dixon, Karin Murris, Joanne Peers,
Theresa Giorza and Chanique Lawrence*

Routledge
Taylor & Francis Group

LONDON AND NEW YORK

Designed cover image: Cover artwork by Lauren Herman

First published 2025
by Routledge
4 Park Square, Milton Park, Abingdon, Oxon OX14 4RN

and by Routledge
605 Third Avenue, New York, NY 10158

Routledge is an imprint of the Taylor & Francis Group, an informa business

British Library Cataloguing-in-Publication Data
A catalogue record for this book is available from the British Library

Library of Congress Cataloging-in-Publication Data
Names: Dixon, Kerryn, author. | Murris, Karin, author. | Peers, Joanne, author. | Giorza, T. (Theresa), author. | Lawrence, Chanique, author.
Title: Postdigital play and global education: reconfiguring research / Kerryn Dixon, Karin Murris, Joanne Peers, Theresa Giorza, and Chanique Lawrence.
Description: Abingdon, Oxon; New York, NY: Routledge, 2024. | Series: Postqualitative, new materialist and critical posthumanist research | Includes bibliographical references and index.
Identifiers: LCCN 2023056061 (print) | LCCN 2023056062 (ebook) | ISBN 9781032070223 (hardback) | ISBN 9781032070278 (paperback) | ISBN 9781003205036 (ebook)
Subjects: LCSH: Education–Philosophy. | Education–Research–Methodology. | Play. | Posthumanism.
Classification: LCC LB14.7 .D59 2024 (print) | LCC LB14.7 (ebook) | DDC 370.1–dc23/eng/20240122
LC record available at https://lccn.loc.gov/2023056061
LC ebook record available at https://lccn.loc.gov/2023056062

ISBN: 9781032070223 (hbk)
ISBN: 9781032070278 (pbk)
ISBN: 9781003205036 (ebk)

DOI: 10.4324/9781003205036

Typeset in Optima LT Std
by Deanta Global Publishing Services, Chennai, India

To the infinite worldings of the children, families, homes and phones, oceans and octopuses of the Children, Technology, and Play project.

CONTENTS

FIGURES AND TABLES

Figures

Tables

ACKNOWLEDGEMENTS

This book would not have been possible without the LEGO Foundation committing itself to fund research projects about children and play. We would like to thank them, and particularly Bo Stjerne Thomsen for his ongoing support of the *Children, Technology and Play* (CTAP) project. Thanks also to Jackie Marsh from The University of Sheffield for inviting us to partner with them. The South African component of this collaborative research project was situated at The University of Cape Town (UCT) and consent for the fieldwork in the schools and the homes was granted by the research ethics committee of the School of Education at UCT and the Western Cape Education Department. Through collaboration with The University of Sheffield's research team, we have learned much and we continue to benefit from ongoing research relationships and collaborative publications.

We would like to express our deep gratitude to all the children and their human and more-than-human families who welcomed us so generously into their homes. The generosity in sharing their playworlds, thoughts, theories, and ideas inspired us to write this book. The hospitality and flexibility of the South African teachers and principals of the schools involved in the CTAP project made it possible for us to do the fieldwork for which we are very grateful. We would also like to thank The Centre for Creative Education for opening their space for our long-awaited CTAP project celebration event with the families we write about in the last chapter.

We appreciate the amazingly talented South African researchers, research assistants, fieldworkers, transcribers, and translators who formed a new research community (and beyond) through playing, writing, swimming, fieldworking, sitting around many tables, knitting, eating, and drinking. A caring and generous research network was formed and further strengthened by new projects, some also funded by the LEGO Foundation.

The theorising and enactment of complex posthumanist philosophies would not have been possible without the ongoing academic conversations and friendships within our weekly Posthumanism Reading Group (see https://www.decolonizingchildhood.org/reading-group).

Our understanding of agential realism has greatly benefited from Karen Barad's seminal book *Meeting the Universe Halfway* (2007), their video presentations, and direct engagement with their ideas during a two-day seminar, organised by the Decolonising Early Childhood Discourses research project (June 10–11, 2017) of which Karen Barad is a member. Karen's visit to Cape Town profoundly affected the research of several South African scholars (see Murris & Bozalek, 2023) including the authors of this book.

A special thanks to Simon Geschwindt for editing this book and George Rowley, research assistant of the Postqualitative Research Collective project (NRF Grant number 129306) for creating the podcasts for the website. Thanks also to the editors of Routledge,

Adam Woods and Matt Bickerton, for their unwavering support, patience, and commitment to this book series, including this book.

The book has benefitted from sections of articles that were published before. Chapter 2's engagement with the Learning Through Play Experience Tool (LtPET) also benefited from our conversations that resulted in an earlier publication (Murris, 2022). Part of Chapter 3 is a rewritten version of Murris and Peers (2022), which has also influenced the conversation in Chapter 4 about the sackball. Chapter 5 draws on Joanne Peers' PhD thesis, "Watery Lives: Relational Bodies of Environmental Education Research." In Chapter 6, some key ideas about Zuko's vignette were published previously in Murris (2022). We would like to thank the anonymous reviewers of these publications for their helpful feedback in strengthening them.

As always such collaborations are impossible without the generous gifts of our human and more-than-human kin and companions and multi-species communities. An undefinable thank you for the unconditional support, patience, wagging tails, cups of tea, accidental Zoom appearances, a last-minute cross-country drive to Cape Town, and being gracious about our absence for family events. To Sean Ramsden, Graham and Brenda Dixon, Hilary Janks, Simon, Delilah and Poppy Geschwindt, Forty, Hope, Grant, Seth and Ben Peers, Nozabathini Ludziya, Thobeka, Botle, Daniella and Junior Mabaso, Trevor and Jackie Canis Africanis, the two Jeanettes—Jeanette Clark and Jeanette Isaacman, Sion Geschwindt, Eliana and Luna Lawrence-Geschwindt, and Susan 'Tietie' Lawrence.

We carry with us the histories and voices of The Cape Flats, Cloetesville Stellenbosch and the foamy and salty waters of Scarborough Beach, St James and Kalk Bay tidal pools, the river, beach and sea in Oulu. These significant bodies of water have helped us manage the high and low tides of research.

It has been a sheer delight to write and illustrate this book together-apart in the postdigital. Co-authoring has been given a different take in our Slow scholarship: playing, worlding, and becoming different(ly) as researcher/authors.

SERIES EDITOR FOREWORD

This book ends with a claim: "The vignettes in the book give an imaginary of how and why large international research projects can be, and should be, designed differently, along *tentacular* rather than straight lines" (p. 215). I begin the foreword with an invitation for us to ponder this statement. What might tentacular research projects look like? What might they do? And why should large international research projects be designed differently, tentacularly? Again, what might this do for our world?

This is the book or research endeavour that we often don't hear about. The left unsaid. The stories that are left on the drawing-room floor, so to speak. Yet, the field of (post)qualitative, and educational research more broadly, is in desperate need of these research stories. *Postdigital Play and Global Education: Reconfiguring Research* is not 'the study' itself but rather the study of the study. The authors re-turn to an international research project, Children, Technology, and Play (CTAP), to open up thinking and research possibilities. This book illustrates the messiness and complexity of doing research.

As readers, we are invited into the authors' doings of inquiry through soundscapes from QR codes, images, and inventive writing such as a chapter written as a transcript.

This book is also much needed as it is situated in the global south and gives life and depth to parts of our globe that aren't always foregrounded in the research machine of academia and publishing. As the authors write, their "questions are entangled with lifeworlds in the global south and hooking into the traumatic geopolitical and spatial realities of living in post-Apartheid South Africa" (p. 154). As I made my way through the book, I was hooked into vignette after vignette about human and more-than-human lives in South Africa. Yet, as the authors remind us, posthuman vignettes are unbounded. And so, I found myself with/in the stories remembering back to my times visiting South Africa, to conversations and relationships with some of the authors, research studies I've been a part of, and my own positions of power and privilege in the world.

In a book series on the doing of postqualitative, new materialist, and critical posthumanist research, this text is a welcome addition as the authors dive into conversations on inquiry processes and practices. They take readers through discussions on data, not as a thing of the past but as open, porous, and generative with every re-turn. Moreover, the entire book is a re-turning to data from the international CTAP project. Perhaps as scholars we could learn to re-turn to data more often rather than be on quests to 'collect' or produce more data, study after study. The authors also invite us to consider concepts such as play and creativity as processes, doings, and transindividual inspired by post-philosophical writings. The authors beg us to consider the (in)visible workings of power and apparatuses of adult-human researchers. And, while other scholars have questioned voice and transcripts, these authors put those insights into conversation with those doing the transcriptions, or transcribers. Finally, the authors dwell on the 'research site'. As they note, surprisingly, research sites are often not discussed in mainstream qualitative research books, and thus ask: why do research sites disappear in textbooks? The authors note this is dangerous as it perpetuates a narrative that places and spaces are apolitical.

Lastly, I admire the authors for advocating loudly that postqualitative research and ethics cannot be pulled apart. Thus, reminding us, we must make writerly and academic spaces to trouble taken-for-granted aspects of doing research and trouble the research studies themselves. I'm grateful that these authors demand for themselves, and all scholars, a sense of accountability and call to ethics to work through complex issues in our inquiry practices, not solely to solve the problem or find answers. Rather, as the authors write, inspired by Donna Haraway, a staying with the trouble of doing inquiry. Research ethics are the every day, perhaps mundane decisions we make in the relationships and events we did(n't) anticipate in our research studies. This artfully written book is an exceptional example about re-turning to research studies and thus, staying with the trouble of (post)qualitative inquiry. They invite us to tentacularly design research studies. Our world needs them.

Candace R. Kuby
Series Co-editor
Columbia, Missouri, USA
December 21, 2023

PREFÁCIO

Nossa busca (de Heloisa da Silva, João Ricardo Viola dos Santos e minha) pela realização de um pós-doutorado na África do Sul (2019–2020) estava ligada a um interesse em estabelecer parcerias e compartilhar estudos dentro do sul global. Brasileiros, nos acostumamos a não nos identificar pelo continente a que pertencemos. Aprendemos cedo que, embora habitemos a América do Sul, "americanos" é um termo reservado para moradores de um país em específico, ao norte. Produzidas por essas e outras marcas, Heloisa da Silva e eu temos trabalhado com história oral fazendo circular na academia vozes que já circulam em outras comunidades, mas que foram sistematicamente silenciadas nas histórias da Educação Matemática, nossa área de formação e atuação[1]. Nessa direção, houve identificação imediata com pessoas e grupos estudantes de Paulo Freire e de teorias decoloniais na Universidade de Cape Town.

A busca pela supervisão de Karin Murris vinculava-se a um interesse em compreender/operar com as potencialidades da perspectiva pós-humanista no contexto sul africano, assim o convite para participação no Children, Technology and Play (CTAP) Project (2019–2020) em parceria com University of Sheffield (UK) e a Fundação LEGO provocou um espanto inicial. É importante ressaltar que o aceite a esse convite se deu por perceber como coletivo esse espanto e por compreender que o lugar de fala das/os pesquisadoras/es envolvidas/os permitiria a produção de e um caminhar com diferentes questões. A preocupação com a localização desse brincar em termos de meio ambiente e relacionalidade como forma de mapear relações entre esse brincar, a criatividade e a aprendizagem e identificar modos como a tecnologia lhe dá formas era, já, um ponto importante na direção de pensar na interseccionalidade de gênero, raça, classe e língua do contexto sul africano após apartheid.

Este livro aborda não somente vazamentos sempre presentes quando uma proposta e um roteiro se afirmam, aborda modos outros de fazer e pensar a pesquisa e sua decorrente produção de performances, temporalidades, mundos. Construído como um convite a olhar, ouvir, observar, tocar, se afetar, articular diferentes emaranhados... este texto opera com textos, imagens e QR Codes que perturbam a tendência de se cristalizar um posicionamento, uma linha única de raciocínio. Tratam-se de vinhetas apresentadas como portas de acesso a outros espaços e produções em aberto, tratam-se de potenciais momentos de captura do leitor, de inter-ferência em modos "acostumados" de pensar.

Por esta razão, um dos primeiros movimentos neste livro é pen-sar as experiências educacionais investigativas nele presentes a partir do sul global. O antropólogo brasileiro Eduardo Viveiros de Castro (2010)[2] provoca aqueles que supõem que todas as cul-turas estão preocupadas com seus "problemas e que existam, sobretudo, para resolvê-los" (p. 3). As experiências narradas neste livro, para além de lidar com as questões de um projeto amplo (seja na direção de responder a elas ou contra elas—Viveiros de

Castro, 2006[3]; como disponível em Marsh et al., 2020[4]), buscam produzir movimentos orientados pela perspectiva pós-humanista e seus modos de interrogar/construir o mundo.

Ao mesmo tempo em que há um cuidado na construção de respiradouros como espaços para produção outra de leitores, há uma preocupação inicial em afirmar linhas fundamentais que emaranham a perspectiva pós humanista exercitada. O que poderia ser tomado como uma prática didática, é por nós entendida como a afirmação política da multiplicidade, um convite a pensar diferente do que se pensa, a caminhar acompanhado por outras questões, uma perturbação (resgatada em diferentes momentos do livro) na tentação globalizante de reconhecer algo a partir de outro já conhecido. É preciso estranhar para conhecer.

As autoras performam um "re-turning" às fontes e análises difrativas que propõem um mapeamento de interferências questionando a noção de escala, e que escapam ao padrão da comparação, uma vez que propõe a leitura através. Esse livro é, assim e também, um convite a conhecer não necessariamente o que se produz de pesquisa a partir de uma metodologia, mas como pesquisa e pesquisadores são produzidos quando se afirma o que tenho chamado de uma sensibilidade metodológica. Um convite a pensar a perspectiva investigativa como política uma vez que esta explicita a não neutralidade de conceitos (como o humano), produz gramáticas e performances com e a partir das quais se fala, pensa e se produz (in)visibilidades. Uma política que, no caso desta obra, questiona a organização binária do mundo e afirma diferentes formas de vida produzidas em emaranhamento.

Por fim, pós-humanismo, pós-digital, pesquisa pós-qualitativa, brincar, aprender ... são abordados por vozes femininas potentes no âmbito acadêmico, o que explicita um lugar de fala (Djamila

Ribeiro, 2017[5]) marcado pelas experiências de ser mulher (em todas as suas interseccionalidades com raça e classe) em um mundo em que conceitos, métodos, gramáticas, currículos ... têm como norma a branquitude, a masculinidade e a heterossexualidade.

Luzia Aparecida de Souza
Federal University of Mato Grosso do Sul-UFMS
Campo Grande, Brazil
December 2023

Notes

1 Somos pesquisadoras vinculadas aos Grupos de História Oral e Educação Matemática- GHOEM (https://www2.fc.unesp.br/ghoem /index2.html) e História da Educação Matemática em Pesquisa-HEMEP (http://hemep.org/).

2 Viveiros de Castro, Eduardo. (2010). O Anti-Narciso: lugar e função da Antropologia no mundo contemporâneo. Revista Brasileira de Psicanálise, versão impressa ISSN 0486-641X, vol.44, no.4, São Paulo.

3 Viveiros de Castro, Eduardo (2006). No Brasil, todo mundo é índio, exceto quem não é. Povos Indígenas no Brasil : 2001–2005 | [editores gerais Beto Ricardo e Fany Ricardo]. (pp. 41-49). São Paulo: Instituto Socioambiental.

4 Marsh, J., Murris, K., Ng'ambi, D., Parry, R., Scott, F., Bishop, J., Bannister, C., Da Silva, H., Dixon, K., Doyle, G., Driscoll, A., Giorza, T., Hall, L., Hetherington, A., Krönke, M., Margary, T., Morris, A., Nutbrown, B., Peers, J., Rashid, S., Santos, J., Scholey, E., Souza, L., Thomsen, B.S., Titus, S., and Woodgate, A. (2020). Children, Technology and Play. The LEGO Foundation.

5 Ribeiro, Djamila. (2017). O que é lugar de fala?. Belo Horizonte: Letramento, 115 p.

PREFACE

Our pursuit (by Heloisa da Silva, João Ricardo Viola dos Santos, and myself) of a postdoctoral experience in South Africa (2019–2020) was driven by an interest in establishing partnerships and sharing studies within the global south. As Brazilians, we have become accustomed to not identifying ourselves solely by the continent to which we belong. We learned early on that, although we inhabit South America, the term 'Americans' is reserved for residents of a specific country to the north. Through our work, Heloisa da Silva and I have been engaged in oral history, bringing voices into academic discourse that already resonate within other communities but have been systematically silenced in the narratives of Mathematics Education, our field of expertise and engagement.[1] In this regard, there was an immediate connection with individuals and student groups associated with Paulo Freire and decolonial theories at the University of Cape Town.

The pursuit of supervision under Karin Murris was linked to an interest in comprehending/engaging with the potentialities of the posthumanist perspective in the South African context.

Thus, the invitation to participate in the Children, Technology and Play (CTAP) project (2019–2020) in collaboration with the University of Sheffield (UK) and the LEGO Foundation initially elicited astonishment. It is crucial to highlight that acceptance of this invitation occurred in recognising the collective nature of our astonishment and the understanding that the place from which the researchers involved spoke, would allow them to produce and move forward with different questions. The concern for situating play in terms of environmental and relational aspects, as a way to map connections between play, creativity, and learning, and to identify how technology shapes it, was already an important point in considering the intersectionality of gender, race, class, and language in the South African context post-Apartheid.

This book not only addresses the ever-present leaks that occur when a proposal and a script are asserted but also explores alternative ways of conducting and conceptualising research and its resulting production of performances, temporalities, and worlds. Constructed as an invitation to look, listen, observe, touch, be affected, and articulate different entanglements, this book operates with texts, images, and QR codes that disrupt the tendency to crystallise a position or a single line of reasoning. These are vignettes presented as gateways to other spaces and open-ended productions, representing potential moments of capturing the reader and interference in 'accustomed' modes of thinking.

For this reason, one of the initial movements in this book is to consider the investigative educational experiences presented within it from a global south perspective. Brazilian anthropologist Eduardo Viveiros de Castro (2010)[2] challenges those who assume that all cultures are concerned with their 'problems and exist, above all, to solve them' (p. 3). The experiences narrated in this book, beyond dealing with the issues of a broad project (whether towards responding to them or against them—Viveiros de Castro, 2006[3]; as discussed in Marsh et al., 2020[4]), aim to generate movements guided by the post-humanist perspective and its ways of questioning/constructing the world.

Simultaneously, while there is careful attention given to the construction of breathing spaces as sites for the alternative production of readers, there is an initial concern in asserting fundamental lines that entwine the exercised posthumanist perspective. What might be considered a didactic practice is understood here as the political affirmation of multiplicity—an invitation to think differently from the norm, to navigate alongside other questions, a disturbance (retrieved at various points in the book) against the globalising temptation to recognise something from what is already known. It is necessary to estrange in order to understand.

The authors perform a "re-turning" to sources and diffractive analyses that propose a mapping of interferences, questioning the notion of scale and escaping the standard of comparison, as they advocate for a reading through. This book is, thus and also, an invitation to understand not necessarily what research produces through a methodology, but how research and researchers are produced when a methodological sensitivity is affirmed. It invites consideration of the investigative perspective as a form of politics, as it explicitly reveals the non-neutrality of concepts (such as the human), generates grammars and performances through and from which one speaks, thinks, and produces (in)visibilities. A politics that, in the case of this work, challenges the binary organisation of the world and asserts different forms of life produced in entanglement.

Finally, posthumanism, postdigitalism, postqualitative research, play, learning … are addressed by powerful female voices in the academic sphere, explicitly revealing a standpoint (Djamila Ribeiro, 2017[5]) shaped by the experiences of being a woman (in all its intersections with race and class) in a world where concepts, methods, grammars, curricula … are normed by whiteness, masculinity, and heterosexuality.

Luzia Aparecida de Souza
Federal University of Mato Grosso do Sul-UFMS
Campo Grande, Brazil
December 2023

Notes

1 We are researchers affiliated with the Oral History and Mathematics Education Groups - GHOEM (https://www2.fc.unesp.br/ghoem/index2.html) and the History of Mathematics Education in Research—HEMEP (http://hemep.org/).

2 Viveiros de Castro, Eduardo. (2010). O Anti-Narciso: lugar e função da Antropologia no mundo contemporâneo. Revista Brasileira de Psicanálise, versão impressa ISSN 0486-641X, vol.44, no.4, São Paulo.

3 Viveiros de Castro, Eduardo (2006). No Brasil, todo mundo é índio, exceto quem não é. Povos Indígenas no Brasil : 2001–2005 | [editores gerais Beto Ricardo e Fany Ricardo]. (pp. 41–49). São Paulo: Instituto Socioambiental.

4 Marsh, J., Murris, K., Ng'ambi, D., Parry, R., Scott, F., Bishop, J., Bannister, C., Da Silva, H., Dixon, K., Doyle, G., Driscoll, A., Giorza, T., Hall, L., Hetherington, A., Krönke, M., Margary, T., Morris, A., Nutbrown, B., Peers, J., Rashid, S., Santos, J., Scholey, E., Souza, L., Thomsen, B.S., Titus, S., and Woodgate, A. (2020). Children, Technology and Play. The LEGO Foundation.

5 Ribeiro, Djamila. (2017). O que é lugar de fala?. Belo Horizonte: Letramento, 115 p.

1

STORYING THE CHILDREN, TECHNOLOGY, AND PLAY (CTAP) PROJECT

The picnic table: storying the project

It is early July 2019. Karin Murris is approached by the University of Sheffield who are conducting a study into young children's play with technology in the UK. They want to do a parallel study in South Africa to offer a perspective from the south. Karin is working at the University of Cape Town (UCT) in early childhood teacher education. The funder, LEGO Foundation, is concerned about the disappearance of play in relation to children's learning across global educational contexts.[1] They are "committed to redefining play and re-imagining learning to ensure children develop the skills needed to navigate an uncertain and complex world" (https://www.legofoundation.com/en /why-play/). They expect that new insights into the characteristics of digital play will help transform pedagogies in education to become more play-based.

There are strong reasons for accepting the invitation. The first is that although there has been an increase in research on African childhoods in recent years, much of this research is characterised

DOI: 10.4324/9781003205036-1

by negative, pessimistic depictions of trauma, marginalisation, and lack (Penn, 2005; Ensor, 2012; Imoh, 2016; Imoh et al., 2022). A substantial body of cross-disciplinary research in the global north includes focused investigations into children's play, and digital play specifically (for some examples see, Burn & Richards, 2014; Marsh et al., 2020; Osgood et al., 2017; Potter & Cowan, 2020; O' Connor et al., 2023; Livingstone & Pothing, 2022), yet there is a paucity of global research into both kinds of play in the global south. African children's contemporary play also receives less attention in global scholarship (Gendron et al., 2022). We know that although African children from no-income or low-income households have limited access to digital technologies in their homes, educational settings, or communities (Lee et al., 2019) we are curious about their digital play. Thirdly, we suspect that our geopolitical context will provide valuable insights into children's play on the other side of the so-called 'digital divide' (Van Dijk & Hacker, 2003; Van Deursen & Helsper, 2015; Kuhn et al., 2023) as well as its impact on education in South Africa (Dixon, 2020; Chisango & Marongwe, 2021).

The invitation coincides with Karin co-presenting with a team of childhood researchers at a three-day conference in Cape Town. Karin calls an impromptu meeting with researchers who might be interested in this project. The gathering includes a mixture of postgraduate researchers, civil society activists, and academics from different South African universities working in early years education.

Sitting on picnic benches, leaning over our plates, we scan the proposed project on printouts spread across the table (see Figure 1.1). The project aims to identify the ways in which technology shapes play in children's play environments; examine the relationship between play, creativity, and learning; and explore adults'

FIGURE 1.1   Huddled around the picnic table

mediating role in digital play (Marsh et al., 2020). The following questions were generated to guide the research:

- What is the relationship between children's use of technology and their play in everyday life?
- What skills and knowledge do children develop in their play with technology?
- What is the relationship between play, technology, and creativity?

- How far does children's play with technology demonstrate the LEGO Foundation's five characteristics of learning through play[2]?
- How do parents and adults facilitate children's play with technology, and what are their views on this issue?
- To what extent is children's play with technology shaped by socio-cultural contexts?

(Marsh et al., 2020, p. 4)

Joanne Peers, an ever-pragmatic teacher-educator and doctoral researcher, comments on the scale of this mixed methods project. Karin will ask a colleague at UCT, Dick Ng'ambi, an expert in Educational Technology, to manage the quantitative part of the project. This entails a large-scale survey, gathering information from parents about children's use of technology across South Africa.

Huddled around the table, the envisaged research design becomes clearer. The qualitative part of the project that focuses on children, their families, and the schools they attend is expected to start in early August leaving us with less than four weeks to get it up and running! A flurry of questions arise about the practicalities of doing this project, drowning out the noisy buzz of other conference delegates. The movement of curious hands and sheaves of paper on the picnic table grows more frantic. It dawns on us that this project is only possible if we constitute sub-teams of people we already know (well). We ask ourselves, 'Who will be available in the coming seven months to be part of the project?' Some people around the table volunteer and other names are mentioned.

The mood is infectious, and it is difficult not to be swept up by the enthusiasm as we start planning. As is inevitable in all large projects, some people do not have the capacity to commit themselves to the project and new people come on board as the project enters different phases.

In the following week Karin forms four sub-teams of fieldworkers. Joanne leads one team. Theresa Giorza, an early childhood researcher and art educator at the University of the Witwatersrand, in Johannesburg, will lead a team there. Kerryn Dixon, a literacy researcher who works with Theresa, takes over leading another team and supports the groups in analysing the data and writing the final CTAP report. Chanique Lawrence, with a background in African studies and Linguistics, is appointed as the lead transcriber and translator in the project. Three researchers from Brazil, Luzia Aparecida de Souza, Heloisa da Silva and João Ricardo Viola dos Santos on a postdoctoral research programme with Karin accept the invitation to join the research project.

The (envisaged) research design for the CTAP project

Voices begin to discuss the project's qualitative requirements. The University of Sheffield's proposed design has four stages and suggests that the project begins in children's homes. At its centre will be ten focus children between the ages of 3 and 11 and their families. Briefly summarised in Table 1.1 the stages are envisaged as follows.

It is critical for us that the families who participate in the study reflect the racial, socio-economic, ethnic, and linguistic diversity of South Africa's population. It is also important that several members of the team either work or live (or both) in the marginalised communities which most of these children come from, giving them 'insider' status in these communities. This is an important consideration because of the intersectional nature of gender, race, language, and class in the South African context and the fact that

TABLE 1.1 Four envisaged stages of data collection for the CTAP project

Stages		Data Collection Methods	Data Collected
Stage 1	Home visits to focus children	• Four to five visits by fieldworkers to observe children playing • Interviews with parents and children • Research diaries for younger children to draw in	• Fieldnotes • Photographs • Video recordings • GoPro footage • WhatsApp conversations • Interview transcripts • Drawings
Stage 2	School visits	• Four classroom observations • Class teacher interview • Four focus group interviews with focus child and peers with participatory activities (making a collage, a concept map, inventing a toy with LEGO and playdough)	• Fieldnotes • Photographs • Video recordings • Concept maps and collages • Interview transcripts
Stage 3	Community visits	• Observation of child at after-school or community activity • Interview with community/after-school lead	• Fieldnotes • Photographs • Video recordings • Interview transcripts
Stage 4	Parent interviews	• 30 in-depth telephonic interviews with parents who completed quantitative survey	• Interview transcripts

racialised demographics still exist in the 'post'-Apartheid context. As it turns out, we work with nine families, because two of the ten focus children are twins. Six primary schools and one preschool agree to take part in the study.

We realise that the envisaged research design requires some changes. Some of these are pragmatic but all are affected by what it means to research in the global south. At multiple points during this project, we are conscious of dominant assumptions that come to light when researching across contexts in the global north and global south. For example, we recognise that all the timelines for the project are designed with the global north school year in mind. UK researchers can start home visits in September with plenty of time to collect data from schools. However, the South African school year runs from January to December, and no research is allowed in state schools in the fourth academic term because of end-of-year assessments. School visits will need to happen before home visits, with tighter timelines.

Dominant assumptions about research procedures and research instruments affect the ways in which data is generated and can be presented. There will be many moments during fieldwork when we realise how these assumptions are in tension with researching children in the global south and how we could have worked differently. These realisations motivated us to write a book that sits with some of these tensions about what it means to do research and how we can tell different stories about research with children in the global south.

What this book is (not) about

This book is *not* an account of the findings from the CTAP research project (for that, see Marsh et al., 2020). The reality of funded research projects and their associated reports is that they are always constrained in terms of time, funder's briefs, scope, and page limits. This book however is also *not* an extended account that builds on some of the findings from the overall project (see e.g., Murris et al., 2022; Scott et al., 2023). For example, we are *not* focusing on parents' perspectives of children's play or findings that deal with identifying the development of children's knowledge and skills through learning through play. Findings that do and do not make it into a report, and the experiences of the research team that live on, continue to resonate long after projects end. Rather than assuming that the life of a project is over when the final report is published, this book *is* a re-turning to the South African data and our experiences of being researchers on the project (see also, Murris, 2022b; Murris & Peers, 2022).

It is important to state that this book is *not* a minority report that undercuts what has already been presented. Rather re-turning is a generative posthumanist methodology worked with extensively by quantum physicist and feminist philosopher Karen Barad. This methodology regards data not as something in the past, closed, and finished when a project has come to an end, but as open and porous and generative in every re-turn. Inspired by the complex everyday practices of an earthworm, Barad (2014, p. 168) proposes re-turning as a non-prescriptive methodology that involves a "multiplicity of processes":

> such as the kinds earthworms revel in while helping to make compost or otherwise being busy at work and at play: turning the soil over and over – ingesting and excreting it, tunnelling through it, burrowing, all means of aerating the soil, allowing oxygen in, opening it up and breathing new life into it.

This book *is* about a re-turning to specks of our data that invoke the down-to-earth practices of the earthworm. Re-*turning* to this project and 'the data' is a means of composing and decomposing: opening it up, letting the air in, allowing it to become different through collaborative readings, thinking-with, re-turning, re-working, re-cognising, and re-configuring.

As a Slow methodology, this is not necessarily about doing things more slowly, but about doing justice (ethics) to the complexity (epistemological) of the world of which we are a part (ontological) (Leibowitz & Bozalek, 2018). In iterative, Slow re-turnings we argue that this project has the potential to radically reconfigure education research.

The approach we have taken to reconfigure education research is located in the teams' experiences of this project. We draw on moments when we were out of step, that chafed, that would not fit neatly into normalised ways of conducting research. We aim to reconfigure research lenses by showing the ways in which they are not innocent (Chapter 3). We open up concepts like 'research data' by challenging the view of interview transcripts as inert (Chapter 4), and 'research sites' as neutral spaces (Chapter 5), that encourage us to ask questions about our responsibility and accountability as researchers.

Through interpreting 'small' things and moments in their specificity and by allowing questions that trouble power-producing binaries 'all the way down', we aim to reconfigure child agency and creativity (Chapters 2 and 6). We propose postdevelopmental accounts of children's 'postdigital' play, thereby reconfiguring humanist notions of play (Chapter 2). Despite the socio-economic, linguistic, ethnic, gender, and racial inequalities, the playworlding of children in South Africa shows that children's creativity within a 'postdigital' world warrants a re-turn. We offer a theoretical contribution to the relatively new concept of the 'postdigital' by challenging who and what can be playful and creative particularly when people live in resource-constrained environments.

Through a series of vignettes (see next section about 'vignette') involving complex human and other-than-human collaborations (e.g., GoPros, a sackball, transcribing software, an octopus, wrestlers, research diaries) we interrupt the Western developmental notions of agency that are currently dominant in research involving young children. Reading data in posthumanist ways has decolonial potential and is a much-needed orientation in global debates about research. We aim to show how different socio-cultural conditions and geopolitical realities offer new insights into education research.

Introducing 'concepts' we work with

In the earlier sections, we mentioned some of the key concepts we work with in this book. Rather than mentioning them in passing and assuming readers are familiar with them, we outline how we understand and enact these concepts, emphasising how they relate to child(ren) and education research. Before we let

post-,

posthumanism,

postdevelopmental,

postcolonial and decolonial

postdigital

nonrepresentationalism,

reconfigure,

and *vignette*

cascade together through this section, we pause a while and think with the concept of 'concept' as a way of opening up another entry point into this book.

A concept is not an abstract notion but a *doing*, a material-discursive practice that makes us do research in particular ways. Meaning-making, which is often centred on the word, is always a specific material doing or enactment, a *performance*. Language is only one particular way of doing and being in the world. The discourses we inhabit shape what is possible and not possible to say and do. Barad (2019a) warns us that concepts are "sedimented[3] ways of thinking … so deep that we hardly question them anymore." Consequently, they come to be regarded as ahistorical and apolitical. Meaning is firmly established through fixed definitions and transmitted through curricula that reproduce hierarchical nesting classifications. For example, 'child' is nested in the concept of the 'human' and the 'human' is nested in the 'species'.

Rather we prefer Deleuze and Guattari's (1994, p. 23) view that "[c]oncepts are centres of vibrations, each in itself and everyone in relation to all others." The notion of 'child' is, for example, inseparable from some obviously connected concepts like 'parent', 'birth', and 'maturation', but the resonances, reverberations, and rebounding of the vibrations connect them to infinite numbers of less obvious ones. (Readers may recognise some coherence with Barad's [2007] notion of diffraction, see pages 71–94.) When making meaning from or with the wholeness of an inseparable reality of connection, we, as human researchers, need to make 'cuts' that foreground certain relations in a particular instantiation of reality. For Barad, then, the smallest unit of analysis can only be an interconnected company of relations rather than an individual object or single identifiable unit like 'child' in a fixed and definable sense.

They, drawing on the philosophy-physics of Neils Bohr, have called this unit of analysis a 'phenomenon' (see Chapter 3 for a detailed discussion).

Regarding concepts in educational research as *performative*, rather than as taken-for-granted or foundational, is an invitation to rethink, re-do, and reconfigure them. It is not about finding something 'pure'. By not taking our conceptual distinctions as foundational or holding them in place, and by always "asking the prior question" and letting them cascade (Barad in Barad & Gandorfer, 2021, p. 18), we keep the questions moving, opening them up and letting the air in—deterritorialising the concepts. For example, by asking 'What is already given ontologically?' and 'What is assumed to be true (*a priori*) before these scientific practices, informed by these theories, get underway?' (e.g., the meanings we bring to what count as 'human' or 'nature' or 'play' or 'digital', or the distinction we make between inanimate and animate bodies).

'Post-' and 'post'

The addition of the concept 'post-' to other core concepts is central in this book. Adding 'post' to other concepts expresses grammatically the posthumanist idea that any 'post' is always in relation to what came 'before'. 'Post' in this book does not indicate 'anti-' or an 'after'. 'Post' does not mean a 'doing away with' or, for example, a 'going beyond' the human ('posthuman-ism'), or 'beyond' qualitative research (postqualitative research), or 'beyond' the developmental (postdevelopmental) or the digital (postdigital). 'Post-' does not suggest a (Cartesian) rupture with the past, a deletion of what has gone on before, or to be replaced by the 'new'.

Like the earthworm (see p. 8), our *postresearch* is about taking 'the past' as porous and 'in front', not 'behind'[4]. This temporal reconfiguring is articulated by our decision not to use the hyphen for key concepts with the 'post' prefix. Unilinear notions such as 'past' and 'future' (as temporalities that follow one another in a line) are problematic in posthumanism. This does not involve a rejection of linear time as such but works with the notion of entangled multiplicities: the 'lines' between past-present-future are entangled in any given moment (Barad, 2007, p. 71). Postresearch for us is about conceptualising events and people as bodies that are neither *in* space nor move *through* time. The past is always already present in the 'here' and 'now' and so are futures (Barad, 2007, 2017c).

Thinking about spacetime relationally is one of the ways that postresearch undoes a binary inherited from Western ontological traditions grounded in Newtonian physics and colonial notions of territory and ownership. Feminist theorists have long pursued relational alternatives to knowing and included "especially the embodied knowledge of women of colour and Indigenous peoples whose cosmologies do not rest upon the binary thinking of Western imperialism" (Fullagar, 2021, p. 120). These ontological binaries have become an intricate part of the grammar of the languages adults use every day and also think with. Barad (2007, p. 5) powerfully sums up some key binaries:

> the social and the natural, the macroscopic and the microscopic, the laws of man and the laws of nature, internal states of consciousness and external states of being, intentionality and history, ethics and epistemology, discourse and materiality.

The relation between discourse and materiality is expressed in postresearch through the notion of 'material-discursive'. Barad (2007,

p. 177) explains that the hyphen between material and discursive indicates that "no priority is given to either materiality or discursivity; neither one stands outside the other." Further unpacking the quotation, implied in the 'intentionality and history' binary is the fact versus fiction bifurcation (what happens in the world versus what is viewed by humans) which opens up a broader understanding of 'storying' as a postresearch methodology. This book is a multiplicity of stories where single stories are always already within and a part of entangled multiplicities. van Dooren and Rose (2016) remind us that telling stories (e.g., about a threatened species of snail in Hawai'i and flying foxes in Australia) is a multidisciplinary act that draws us into different ways of making sense of the worlds of others (including the more-than-human). Our research stories are always already a part of other stories: those of octopuses, oysters, whales, and migratory birds.

The disruption of the macro[5] and micro and inner and outer binaries trouble Newtonian conceptions of time and space as containers and bodies as bounded. Disrupting unilinear time and by re-turning to 'past' data, we allow data to become different by asking questions that trouble the power-producing binaries currently shaping our ethics, epistemologies, and ontologies. A postqualitative approach to 'data' is not abandoning qualitative research, but working differently with data—opening up what counts as data. Data is not treated as "raw", "brute", "inert", "passive", "simple", "concrete" and "lifeless", waiting to be "collected", "extracted" and "coded", in order to be analysed, interpreted, theorised, or used as evidence (Koro-Ljungberg et al., 2018, p. 463). In this book, we enact how "data/empirical material, world and researcher are all part of the same world" (Juelskjaer et al., 2021, p. 146).

A crucial part of this 'post-' work is to re-turn to the concept of the 'human', and what counts as 'fully human', especially what it means to be a 'young human'. It is of significance that even in postresearch, not only Indigenous peoples but also (the) child is often 'forgotten'. For example, when arguing that not only humans are 'intelligent', what tends to be assumed is that *adult* humans are being referred to and not young children and their knowledge claims (Murris, 2022a). In this book, we argue instead that postresearch should question its assumptions about 'the human' that it takes as implicit—even in its rejection. We use the concept 'Adult' with a capital 'A' to indicate its power over child in the Adult/child binary. In academia, the way in which (the) child human is theorised has shifted significantly, especially since poststructuralist and postmodernist childhood scholars' articulation of their postdevelopmental theorisations of child and childhood. It is to them we re-turn after articulating a posthumanist agenda.

Posthumanism

Posthumanism allows us to see how theories, practices, everything, is/are always in relation. But not always and reliably in or part of the same relations. It follows that we cannot generalise about ways of doing or knowing things, or about groups of people. Resisting the impulse to generalise is a challenge for research because of the substantialising work that language does (Barad, 2007; Braidotti, 2013). The grammar of language (with its object and predicate structure) brings into existence figurations of the human as a substance with an essence and a self-contained identity. This in turn determines how agency, causality, and therefore play are conceptualised in education research.

Working with what it means to be human often foregrounds identity and applies criteria of difference in problematic ways. Posthuman and decolonial scholars tell us that the concept of human is not neutral but deeply racialised, sexualised, and genderised (Braidotti, 2013, 2022). Individualism, human-centred and neuro-typical notions of intelligence already built into the concept of the human (and the child) require troubling. Setting humans against animals results in an oversimplified distinction. Criteria of difference are always embedded in power relations: who gets to decide what criteria are used?

The posthuman move to decentre the human is an ontological re-working of relationality by rejecting oversimplified and non-relational notions of the human as *a priori*. Still, it does so without claiming that the human doesn't matter. For Barad (2007, p. 352), the concept 'human' does not refer to individual things (objects) with inherent properties in the world, for example, with agency or with "the ability to engage in cognitive functions that make the universe intelligible" but to phenomena. Various analyses in this book will give a flavour of what this is like.

Posthuman subjectivity is unbounded and embedded. For example, when considering child, it is impossible to say where 'child' ends, and 'Adult' starts or vice versa, or to refer to childhood as a phase in a human's life. A posthumanist conception of childhood disrupts the idea that childhood is temporally and spatially located and simply a characteristic of a young human being of a particular age. Adults can be childlike and child (as in 'childing'). Childhood is not something humans grow out of and can leave behind (Murris & Kohan, 2021). For posthumanists the 'human' materialises, differently, over time, through continuous, diverse, and repetitive processes of enacting specific norms that become expressed as part of the particular enactment or phenomenon. However, these specific norms of what makes a human (set against what constitutes an animal) and the notion of degrees of human-ness, bring structurally into existence the less-than-fully-human (Snaza, 2013, p. 41). Indeed, the critical question in terms of power seems to be, 'Am I human enough?' which is of particular importance for research with children.

Postdevelopmental

Postdevelopmental approaches respond to how the construct of *development* creates and reinforces binaries, not only between Adult/child, but also North/south. Concepts of 'progress', 'maturity', and 'growing up' underpin development. The idea that children need to progress, mature, and grow up to be more knowledgeable and reliable when making claims about their experiences is built into most modernist pedagogies and research practices. The roots of this 'develop-mentality' can be traced back to Ancient Greek Philosophy with Aristotle's exhortation that the individual child's mind/psyche (and body) is in the process of being formed in accordance with its innate natural potential (Stables, 2008). Plato's influence on Descartes resulted in his (now) infamous dualism, which fundamentally shapes developmental theories' prioritisation of the mind/psyche/intellect over the body. The ideal norm (the) child needs to develop into is that of the rational, autonomous Adult.

Jean Piaget's 'genetic epistemology' is a textbook example of how these ideas about child development are naturalised in the epistemologies and methodologies of education research.

The assumption of innate development finds realisation in identifiable universal 'phases' and 'stages', with 'milestones' that measure physical, socio-emotional, artistic, cognitive growth, and language acquisition (Moss & Dahberg, 2005) placing children at the bottom of the intellectual hierarchy (Jenks, 2005).

In a move that indicates that 'post' is not 'anti-' or 'doing away with', some postqualitative researchers suggest a productive re-turning of Piaget's work. For example, Theresa Aslanian (2018) argues that Piaget's intention was purely scientific and not meant to be prescriptive (see also, Murris, 2016). Cristina MacRae (2022) re-turns to Piaget's notion of the sensory-motor, seeing it not as an inferior rung on the ladder. Counteracting the influence the socio-cultural turn has had in education, she suggests that foregrounding the sensory-motor and the body would add more weight to the biological, the physical, and the material dimensions of play and at the same time:

> trouble the idea of play as normatively mapping a pre-determined trajectory where the sensory-motor is both cast as essential and necessary, but *only as a more primitive and unthinking mode that is superseded by reason and the symbolic.*
>
> *(MacRae, 2022, p. 330; our italics)*

At the heart of postdevelopmental research is also the disruption of what philosopher Alfred North Whitehead ([1925] 1948, p. 77) has called the nature-culture bifurcation. Developmentalism assumes that the child equated with nature has to be 'filled' by culture (e.g., knowledge and information), or 'allowed to unfold', or 'interacted with', according to the educator. Thus, it is imperative to ask the prior questions about the ontological relationship between nature and culture, and not simply start with the split between the human and the more-than-human as *given*—what Whitehead proposes is both *non-anthropomorphic* and *non-anthropocentric*. Decentring the (Adult) human from our accounts of what we know and can know (epistemology) is a gesture towards the inclusion of the more-than-human in knowledge-making practices. It is not coincidental that reconfiguring the concept of nature is at the heart of decolonising approaches to education research and childhood. Postcolonial and decolonial are core concepts for a book on post-digital play and it is to these we now turn.

Postcolonial and decolonial

Postcolonial and decolonial theories have an important role to play in this book in terms of what it means to do research. The research we conducted could be understood as being 'located' in the global south but the research design and analysis are shaped by global north orientations. Comaroff and Comaroff (2012) remind us that we need to think about the concept of the global south beyond the geographical binary of the Northern and Southern Hemispheres. The global south can be seen to exist in the global north and vice versa with porous lines between them. The concept is not fixed, but inchoate, not to be defined *a priori* but relationally where its "content is determined by everyday material and political practices" (2012, p. 127). A southern perspective then is not an acknowledgement that we speak for 'the south', as if it were a knowable, monolithic entity, in the same way as it is impossible to say where the west starts and the east begins. Rather our southern perspective is informed by postcolonial, decolonial, and posthuman orientations that trouble dominant Western discourses and practices and that offer ways of working with marginalised communities in the north and south.

Core to the decolonial turn is a move away from the view that decolonisation relates to a historical event where countries became politically independent from colonial rule. The west and the rest of the world continue to be shaped by the "logic, metaphysics, ontology and matrix of power" that are the ongoing products of coloniality (Maldonado-Torres, 2016, p. 10). Decoloniality is a way, Maldonado-Torres continues, of "breaking hierarchies of difference that dehumanise subjects and communities and that destroy nature" (Maldonado-Torres, 2016, p. 10). Decoloniality works with other ontologies through alternative discourses, knowledges, practices.

Baradian posthumanism also breaks with 'hierarchies of difference' by challenging Western individualised subjectivity. The latter sets up the Human as superior, defining it against what it means to be 'animal': 'rational', sophisticated ('tamed'), and is the norm for the exclusion of the irrational, wild, and immature. These power differentials are expressed through binary logic where the human on the left-hand side of the forward slash has power over the human on the right-hand side: Man/woman, Able/disabled, Middle class/working class, Rich/poor, White/black, Adult/child. Human exceptionalism is also enacted in Man's ontological superiority in relation to the material world. Human optics and the way we 'access the world' through Man's knowledge depends on His senses and cognition with a mind that exists separately and very differently from His body. Moreover, this normative Male, able, heterosexual body is individualised and physically and metaphorically contained by His (white) skin. The Subject with His 'inner' and 'outer' experiences is the figuration that makes it possible to *dicho-timise* what is alive and dead, animate or inanimate and exists 'in' this empirical world or as a metaphysical entity (e.g., as a spirit). All of these concepts and their complex entanglements are at stake in this book.

Colonial logics are also deeply implicated in constructions of child, childhood, and developmentalism itself. The Culture/nature binary finds fertile ground where the intellectual development of child stands in for the development of the species (with the child as nature, as the origin of the species) who starts as 'savage' and becomes 'civilised'. The idea that children develop by nature in determinate ways and cannot be hastened is particularly resilient in education. There is nothing 'natural' about childhood (Nandy, 1987). All biological categorisations and appeals to child's 'nature' are political and ethical (Kennedy, 2006) and bound up with how we conceptualise the Human. Our modern understanding of child and childhood is also racialised (Oswell, 2013). Adultism and racism work in colonising ways projecting "an autonomous (white) adult" onto "the (white) child" thus globalising the Western figure of the child (Biswas, 2022, p. 13).

Toby Rollo (2018) takes this further by arguing that the concept of childhood itself is the internal logic that has made colonial superiority and the notion of the ontological 'other' possible. Adult humans use the logic of childhood to place themselves above nature and to justify not only the colonisation of children but also land and natural resources. It is this binary logic that makes it possible to treat an entire continent such as Africa as a child in need of development.

Postcolonial and posthuman writings challenge the ways in which Enlightenment thinking has impacted the Human researcher in positivist science. Conceptualised through Newtonian notions of space and time, research scientists are viewed as individual, bounded entities who are separate from the objects of their study, and thus, capable of 'objectivity' (Haraway, 1997). Relational ontologies with strong connections to Indigenous cosm(ont)ologies offer alternative ways of knowing and being. Nxumalo (2019) illustrates this relational ontology with her example of African clan names. Clan names connect humans to land, places, ancestors, the living and non-living, pasts and futures, the physical and spiritual. Le Grange (2018) draws attention to the ecological, more-than-human doings of some key African Indigenous philosophies. Bodies are thus unbounded, entangled, and do not exist prior to relations. This is a move away from identities and reconfigures agency. Although situated, this kind of agency is fluid and not socially, geographically, or temporally located in space or time (Barad, 2007, pp. 470–471 ftn 45) as we demonstrate across the chapters.

Postdigital

The concept of the postdigital and postdigital play are developed in greater detail in Chapter 2. As with the other post concepts outlined here, it is important to repeat that the 'post' in 'postdigital' does not point to a time *after* the digital, rather it foregrounds how the digital and the analogue are always already in relation (Apperley et al., 2017; Knox, 2019). Tavin et al. (2021) see the postdigital as looking both back and forward. They give a useful example of the invention of printing technology as a new form of communication. Developed in China in the 11th century and only later in Europe in the 15th century, this printing technology facilitated the transformation of societies and as such pointed towards ever-new and emergent futures. From these technologies emerge the text-based information world we live in with its libraries, universities, forms of teaching and learning, and knowledge management systems.

The digital is based on and grew out of the latent potentialities of these technologies and ensuing cultural systems for creating and managing knowledge that emerges from them. At the same time, new evolutionary forms emerge in changing media conditions that in turn alter cultural forms and societal structures. The postdigital is thus both open-ended and emergent, and part of the shifting material-discursive entanglements in the world. The world is unavoidably digital.

This postdigital orientation has implications for how we consider questions of knowledge and methodology in educational research. In considering postdigital research, Jandric et al. (2022) see the postdigital as epistemically anarchic (drawing on Feyerabend's 1970/1993 term), arguing that as an unbounded concept, postdigital research should not be located within particular disciplinary boundaries or research methods. Rather, its ability to move in transdisciplinary ways and apply different research methodologies challenges the nature of disciplinary boundaries and research approaches. They see the epistemic move to take ownership of concepts by pinning meaning down to be an example of knowledge capitalism. Instead, they call for a postdigital community "to be open to everyone who does good work—including non-human agents" where "knowledge is a common construct and a common good characteristic for knowledge socialism" (Jandric et al., 2022, para 14).

As postresearchers whose backgrounds are in different disciplinary areas, this awareness of who and what is part of the postdigital community is a more response-able way of doing research that values difference. For us, knowledge is always co-constituted and co-created—it is a worlding practice.[6]

In the process of researching and writing this book, creating knowledge is a material-discursive doing and inherently playful. In a project on play, it is impossible not to be affected by play as an impulse and energetic force moving across and among the data. Through our research experiences we have come to know things differently by returning to and reconfiguring them through the possibilities inherent in the digital (e.g., we have produced multiple iterations of data in digital and material form as files of concept maps, research diaries, or fieldnotes that have been shared, saved, misfiled, and uploaded online; we experienced pleasure listening to multiple recordings from multiple devices of single play events; we have been affected by the creative potential offered by AI art generators, and editing software that creates new texts and knowings; we have been immersed in the lively chaos of writing together online across time zones).

In the same way as posthumanism challenges binaries, and the postdigital moves between binaries of the digital and analogue, online and offline, postdigital play challenges us to see beyond the Adult/child binary. It is not just children who play with technology. Like the earthworm that revels in busy work and play, postdigital play reconfigures play events as Baradian *phenomena*, shifting the focus from the humanist understandings of how human bodies use technological devices.

All 'post' concepts we have looked at so far in this chapter have a critical response to core binaries that shape our ontologies and knowledge-making practices. What postqualitative research practices have in common is that they are non-representational, which is the next concept that unfolds.

Nonrepresentationalism

Representational ontologies position humans above or outside the world, assuming an independent and *external* world of subjects and objects that can be known *representationally* and cognitively through ideas and concepts *inside* the human mind. The consequence is the separation of humans from nature (Culture/nature). This way of thinking is "deeply entrenched within Western culture" (Barad, 2007, p. 48) and presupposes that thinking is about representing, measuring, calculating, mapping, and picturing a world that is given or simply 'there'. The other than human is by the very same token posited as an inert, passive substance. Colebrook (2020) also rejects a relationship to thinking (and the 'other') that focuses on the Human claim to exceptionalism and the epistemic arrogance of locating knowledge, intelligence and meaning-making in the subject and only in the human subject. An examination of the position of the scientist is a particularly important trope in considerations of knowledge and thought in postresearch.

Haraway's (1992, 1997, 2016) work is central to the shift to non-representational[7] research. Her work problematises the taken-for-granted position of the scientist in terms of knowledge production. Haraway's feminist critique of the 'objective eye' of the (male) scientist proposes the situatedness of knowledges. The particular positionality of the researcher, with gender, race, and class (and, and, and …) as markers of difference, produces different knowledge. The recognition of 'other' ways of knowing does not stop with the human. Nor does it assume the primacy of language in knowledge production.

Encounters of human and more-than-human elements in the research event changed Haraway's focus from a reflexive practice producing insights, interpretations, and understandings to a de-centred noticing of the event itself. This ontology upsets the possibility for an assumed 'mirroring' between reality and its representation, or between the viewer and 'viewed'. Neither is independent of the other and in each relational encounter both are implicated and 'at risk', always subject to change and being changed.

Haraway critiques qualitative research practices that aim to reflect increasingly accurate or insightful interpretations of already existing realities (collected data; interview transcriptions etc.). She introduces the concept of diffraction as an alternative practice and research methodology. Diffraction recognises the implicatedness of the researcher together with the other human and more-than-human components of the event in the production of the data itself and the co-production of knowledge. Diffraction does justice ontologically to a world that is not made up of fixed, independently definable entities or objects. Rather, reality *is* a continuously changing pattern of 'things' already in relation.

Barad's agential realism builds on Haraway's work on diffraction. They introduce the concept of intra-action. Different from *interaction*, in which component parts of the encounter have separate identities that exist prior to the mixing, in *intra-action*, subjectivities are formed through it—in an agential cut (Barad, 2007, p. 175). Subject and object are entangled in a non-dualist mutually affecting agency in which differences produce difference. An agential cut makes visible an in/separability of co-constituting subject-object; nature-culture; theory-practice; material-discursive. Understanding knowledge-making as part of a *worlding* process has implications for how we do postresearch.

Agential realism troubles the idea that a research design is a politically neutral apparatus that helps observe, record, and measure *what is happening* in a 'research site' objectively. The instruments used to 'collect' data in the CTAP project are our apparatuses: surveys, interviews, observations, measuring scales, and focus groups. Apparatuses are constituted through particular —not just human—nature-culture practices and researchers are not just 'outside' observers of apparatuses. This complexifies what it means to decentralise the (child)human in posthumanist research.

In early childhood education and childhood studies, and therefore relevant for our postresearch on postdigital play, there has been a real interest in research practices that are nonrepresentational. This postresearch reconfigures the figure of (the) child with all its complexities (see, e.g., Murris & Osgood, 2022) by troubling discourses that position the less-human—child—as lacking the following attributes by their very nature (essence): responsibility, maturity, trustworthiness, natural goodness, experience, rationality. Adults (educators, therapists, social workers, and so forth) are put in charge to intervene in the 'natural' processes that have left child wanting (Murris, 2016; Murris & Reynolds, 2018). However, these concepts are 'apparatuses' (Murris, 2022a) that have materialised into particular figurations of child. 'Developing child' is a powerful figuration or representation that dominates the discourses of 'child development', school 'readiness', and age appropriateness and connects with colonial, psychological, and scientific constructions of child and 'other'. Rather than being a neutral descriptor, it works to co-produce self-fulfilling deficit subjectifications (Murris, 2016).

It is apposite in this section of cascading concepts that the concept of *reconfiguring* vibrates with the other 'post-' concepts discussed here. Like re-turning, reconfiguring is an active process in our postqualitative research methodology that enables a reterritorialising of educational research (and research practices more generally), child agency, and humanist notions of play.

Reconfiguring

Critical posthumanist Rosi Braidotti (2002) uses the term 'figurations' as an alternative to metaphors. She sums up her various "critical figurations" in her latest book and the work they do to counter the power of Western philosophy and higher education, advanced capitalism and modern technologies on knowledge production (Braidotti, 2022, p. 213). Figurations (such as 'posthuman child'[8] or the 'nomadic subject') are not "figurative ways of thinking, but rather more materialistic mappings of situated, or embedded and embodied positions" (Braidotti, 2011, p. 13). These subject positions are hybrid, multi-layered, often internally contradictory, interconnected, and weblike. They are not metaphors, but social-material positions: "living maps, a transformation account of the self" (Braidotti, 2011, p. 14) and are "'thinking aids', that help us work through complex issues". Unlike metaphors, figurations demand a sense of "accountability for one's locations" and a "self-reflexivity" that "relies upon a social network of exchanges" (Braidotti, 2002, p. 69). The use of figurations is not an individual activity, but an intra-active process, "the mutual constitution of entangled agencies" (Barad, 2007, p. 33), that is helpful in dismantling scientific objectivity, without giving up on objectivity altogether. By including the more-than-human and other means of response-able knowing, objectivity itself is reconfigured (Barad, 2007). This makes it possible to remain scientifically credible in our pursuit of relationally constructing alternative modes of knowing that include affect and empathy (Braidotti, 2022, p. 216).

In this book some of the concepts we reconfigure are the 'digital', 'play', 'research sites', 'data', 'agency', 'creativity', and 'research' in education.

Vignettes

In this book, vignettes form part of our postqualitative methodology. Vignettes have long been used in research as a means of collecting data in the form of simulations of events for participants to respond to; as a way for researchers to reflect on their research challenges; or to document data. Ely et al. (1997, p. 70) provide a detailed description of vignettes:

> Vignettes are compact sketches that can be used to introduce characters, foreshadow events and analysis to come, highlight particular findings, or summarise a particular theme or issue in analysis and interpretation. Vignettes are composites that encapsulate what the researcher finds through the fieldwork. In every case, vignettes demand attention and represent a growing sense of understanding about the meaning of research work.

The posthuman 'vignettes' in this book demanded attention. We noticed them early on, entangling themselves in our meetings as a way to tell stories with multiple narratives that re-emerge across and beyond the book through intra-connected webs of meaning. They are a non-subjective worlding. As they carried us into the writing they resisted being pigeonholed as "compact sketches" or as summaries of particular themes or issues as Ely et al. (1997) suggest in the quote above. Instead, they enact a performing-with. Performing-with vignettes is an act of reconfiguring: a movement beyond static and bounded linguistic descriptions designed to capture events. For us, to use Haraway's (2016, p. 35) oft-used phrase "it matters what worlds world worlds. It matters what stories tell stories."

Posthuman vignettes are unbounded. They move between, across, and off pages. We never quite knew where they would take us in their iterative becomings. Like photographic vignettes whose edges are darkened or in shadow, these vignettes resist being put in their place with beginnings and endings. They do not only 'foreshadow' the pasts that are enfolded in them. Their indeterminate 'edges' are a reminder of the ways in which our research lenses, like different camera lenses, are implicated in what comes to be focused on, what Barad (2007) would refer to as *agential cuts* (see in particular the vignettes in Chapter 3). Agential cuts affirm and sediment the always already existing relations—unlike Cartesian cuts that separate, cut apart, and dichotimise (Barad, 2014). Posthuman vignettes "expand the ontologies of knowing/becoming/doing by decentring humans and taking the pulse of the flows between humans, nonhumans, and more-than-humans" (Lemieux, 2021, p. 494).

The vignettes in this book are a transmodal compos(t)ing of photographic images, interview transcripts, audio files, video, material artefacts, memories, places, time, atmospheres, and humans coming together to co-create data in the form of open-ended stories with multiple meanings. Going beyond a representational purpose, the stories perform in our research to pull us in and invite us to re-turn (as in turning over) and to re-visit and story differently. We aim to create stories that "hold open possibilities and interpretation and refuse the kind of closure that prevents others from speaking or becoming" (van Dooren & Rose, 2016, p. 85). These stories are agentic, along with ourselves, the child(ren), the more-than-human devices and apparatuses and the spaces and places of the research project.

These posthuman vignettes are postdigitally playful. They are invitations to readers to look, listen, watch, sense, touch, become affected, re-story, and articulate different entanglements by accessing, for example, the QR codes that are part of some vignettes. They take different forms: a comic, diffracted images, soundscapes, and written narratives that weave themselves across and through the chapters. The written narratives are italicised and indented, incorporating other textual data, for readers who choose not to read linearly but want to dip in and out of the storying. The affective waves produced by the emerging vignettes create patterns of difference for all the intra-acting agencies.

The dining room table at Scarborough

Laptop, notebooks, pens, and mugs spread across the wooden dining room table in a house at Scarborough, a small seaside suburb in Cape Town. A group of us from the project are together for the weekend in March 2020. We are talking about what we want to do now that the report is submitted. Chairs accommodate bodies around the table. The CTAP child research participants Della and Linton, Eshal, Henry, Zuko, Sophia, Karabo, Lulama, Kamden, Gemina, Fahiemah, and their families are at the table with us and warming us up as the sea breeze flows through the house. Macro bodies stored in micro digital format whisper material-discursive stories. Photographs, audio files, videos, and transcripts tell multiple stories—so far without an audience (yet). Should we write a book (Figure 1.2)?

FIGURE 1.2 The dining room table at Scarborough

A GoPro camera nestles in a harness against Della's chest. Theresa re-members the feel of the camera and the harness cradling it as her fingers turn the camera on. It begins to record a game of WWE 2K17 that Della and her sister Bongi play on their PlayStation. WWE 2K17 is a digital game created under license from World Wrestling Entertainment, formerly released as *SmackDown!* The children refer to it as SmackDown and we use these titles interchangeably. Through diffractive readings of this vignette, play emerges as an enigmatic and shape-shifting force that flows among and conspires with human and more-than-human agentic becomings: a boundaryless intra-action of old and new technologies, senses, bodies, thoughts, and events. A reconfiguring of the concepts of play and the postdigital in Chapter 2 sees postdigital play as a worlding process that enables a re-turning to play events in later chapters.

The GoPro camera re-turns in Chapter 3. It (accidentally) records a walk back from the shops during a home visit. Walking through a forest of zinc houses in the informal settlement where he lives, Henry's legs nimbly negotiate the narrow metal spaces, money jingling through the movement on sandy pathways. The sound of a roll of sticky tape coming to an end was the impetus to get bodies moving to buy more tape to finish making a sack ball. We re-member how the 'lines' between past-present-future(s) are entangled in these lively moments. We are visited by the haunted moments of research as we re-member how the creative making of the ball is also entangled with our political discomfort and the ethical dilemmas that arose from home visits and decisions to use research 'instruments' that Eshal, Henry's friend, asks us to account for.

We wonder about assumptions in the notion of a 'home visit'. How does the history of home visits affect its realisation as a research practice? Home visits. Home visits with their feudal roots, Judeo-Christian notions of charity, the 'friendly visits' of upper- and middle-class (women) in the 18th and 19th centuries imposing bourgeois notions of morality and behaviour to the poor and working classes (Astuto & Allen, 2009; Winter & Cree, 2016). Home visits as modern institutionalised practices embedded in Western health care, early childhood, and criminal justice systems—a Foucauldian *surveillance* of the less-than-human sick, mad, child, mother, criminal. Home visits that are also shaped by disciplines like anthropology whose early ethnographies cannot escape colonial notions of the 'other' as observable objects with taken-for-granted assumptions about the right of access.

The GoPro camera has its own complex story to tell. Framed as an innovative tool for doing research with children it is not merely an object children can capture their play with, as the original design envisaged. GoPro cameras, like other research instruments, are not innocent or neutral lenses and can cause profound ethical problems in resource-constrained environments. Drawing on a video clip Chapter 3 shows how visual data of Henry can be analysed as (Baradian) phenomenon rather than as a research object or research subject.

A fluffy, hand-knitted yellow jumper knitted by Karin for her daughter in the 1970s covers a small body in a pink Babygro. The jumper is an intragenerational garment that has been passed down from child to child and leaves threads on our skins as a gurgling Eliana moves between laps and arms around the table. She is another member of the research team. A member who was a foetus at the time of the project. Eliana's presence infuses the transcripts, sharing Chanique's body, blood, and thoughts, hearing the soundscapes of the audio recordings as her mother's fingers carefully type transcripts, bringing them into the world.

Words hold a privileged position in the world. In qualitative research, words dominate what constitutes research data. These words are used to represent the worlds researchers construct. But not everyone's words are heard, not everyone's words or languages are considered important enough to be transcribed. In returning to trouble research data, using the example of research transcripts, Chapter 4 brings us and the sack ball from Chapter 3 together in conversation with one another. A postdigital and posthuman perspective foregrounds the value of listening to soundscapes beyond words, of not ignoring affective connections. It shows the generative possibilities that arise when the role of transcriber is recognised as more than outsourced labour but a full member of the research team who is deeply entangled with history and community whose voices live on and in recording devices and digital files.

The briny smell of the air stings our nostrils as the wind whips around us. We walk along the road and down to the beach. The brave amongst us enter the icy water. Where does the beach end and the sea begin? There are no clearly demarcated lines, no boundaries here. There are no beginnings and endings. The sea and beach are enfolded into each other sometimes gently and sometimes in a thrashing churn. What happens when we think about research sites not as bounded entities, containers for human activity but as part of a set of ongoing relations? What happens when we acknowledge how home, school, and community sites affect the collecting and the creation of data?

The sea flanks Eshal as she walks to and from school every day. It accompanies her to the library and up the stairs pouring out in a picturebook she shares with Joanne. It's part of the mesh-work of lines that emerges (Ingold, 2011, 2015), becoming a form of digital play captured in WhatsApps that include tidal pools, swims, visits to the beach, a library, and an octopus. Chapter 5 works with the movements in-between, histories hidden in the liminal. It shows an ongoing worlding that spills over neatly demarcated boundaries, it asks us to rethink linear notions of time and space and in doing so moves us beyond conventional notions of 'research site'.

The ghostly presences of pearl gloves, wrestlers, PlayStations, costumes, GoPros, LEGO, and the Learning through Play Experience Tool (LtPET) flicker across the table. These flick-erings are the in/visible relations diffracted through time, a temporal diffraction ('hauntology', see Derrida, 1994[9]) enacted across spacetime(s). Chapter 6 presents two vignettes that arose from 'sticky data' (MacRae et al., 2018), data that stuck out, stuck itself into diaries, fieldnotes and cameras, and stuck to us with affective intent when we think about child agency and creativity. This chapter provides a postdevelopmental account of child agency and creativity in research design and analysis. In Western thought, agency tends to be attributed to a human being (body) with the capacity to act. Action is often concep-tualised in a narrow sense and in terms of *intentionality*: the agent's mental states, conscious intentions, reasons and events *cause* the action. Creativity in turn is discursively framed as a valued enactment of individual agency. A postdevelopmental view of creativity is not a quality possessed by an individual human who has creative qualities but is distributed and includes the nonhuman, such as technology, land, wind, atmosphere, sound, smell, national curricula, international benchmark testing etc. Rather, it is a force or energy that emerges as new and unexpected links, connections, relations, and effects are produced.

The first vignette is a vignette of a play event that involves Zuko and we diffract the LtPET tool through it. While the LtPET tool is designed to measure the creativity and agency of a child, a relational view of creativity and agency shifts the focus from human competencies and skills. This analysis centres around agency 'without a subject' and paints a more complex picture of who or what can be playful (Haynes & Murris, 2019). The leather, feathers, and pearls vignette takes seriously the call of materials (Bennett, 2010) as part of knowing with "the bling of the living world" (Haraway in Mitman, 2019, p. 19). It brings up intense disturbances of diffracting energies that include digital play, drawing, games, and creative production.

In the final chapter, we choose not to present a set of fixed conclusions or decontextualised 'tips for researchers'. Rather, we propose tentacular moves for postdigital research by drawing attention to the openings and movements produced in and through the chapters.

We end this chapter with a postdigital visual vignette of the entangled relations of the project and sticky data that carries within it stories of postdigital play that we take up in the next and then succeeding chapters that are all written collaboratively (Figure 1.3).

FIGURE 1.3 Visual play with sticky data

Notes

1 See: https://learningthroughplay.com/explore-the-research
2 The Learning through Play Experience Tool (LtPET) is discussed in more detail in Chapters 2 and 6.
3 We put the concept of sedimenting to work by diffracting through Barad's notion of sedimenting. They write that sedimenting is "less about layers or an archeological under-standing of depth, and more about the dynamism according to which even that which is thought to be the lowest level (where questioning stops) iteratively gets brought up to the surface, as it were, and is reworked. Making-sense is very much about touching and aerating. It is about concepts being in touch in their making-sense—in mate-rializing certain matters, and not others, in their excluding of certain matters, and not others—and about the enabling of a response, aerating and breathing. Response-ability is about attending to, tracing, and taking account of entangle-ments, about being in touch with world's practices of materializing/making-sense, including its material-discursive 'concepting'" (Barad in Barad & Gandorfer, 2021 p. 31).
4 This is also how we understand the concept post-Apartheid—as not behind, but always part of the present and future/s.
5 Karen Barad does not claim that scale doesn't matter, but it simply is not a given. They explain that "there is no scale at which the laws of physics change from quantum physics to Newtonian physics, from 'microworld' to 'macroworld'; to the best of our knowledge, quantum physics holds at all scales" (Barad, 2017a, p. G118 ftn 10).
6 Drawing on both Haraway (2016) and Barad (2007), we see worlding as a "non-subjective notion of knowing-with, and becoming-knower [that] requires a sense of the intra-active agency of human and non-human, organic and inorganic entanglements of the world coming to know itself: its 'worlding' (Barad 2007)" (Giorza, 2021, p. 82). See Chapter 2 for a discussion of play as a worlding practice.
7 For an extensive overview of the differences between representa-tional and nonrepresentational research without setting up a binary between the two see Murris & Zhao (2022).

8 Braidotti herself does not use 'posthuman child' but 'posthuman' as a figuration. In fact, child and childhood does not feature at all in her work as part of the critical posthuman project and is only mentioned in the context of women and childcare (see also concern raised about this in Murris, 2022a).

9 Hauntology for Derrida (1994) is a conversation with 'ghosts' in order to reconfigure a different future where the past is not left behind, but already entangled with the present and not yet futures. Barad diffracts through Derrida's notion and acknowledges the influence of Astrid Schrader on their reconfiguring of ontology as a non-human-centred hauntology. For Barad, in an ongoing commitment to questions of justice, hauntology brings to the fore that diffraction is not only about multiple spaces, but also involves multiple temporalities and needs to be introduced into the very construction of each concept, including 'being' and 'time' (Schrader, 2012).

2

THE 'POST' IN POSTDIGITAL PLAY

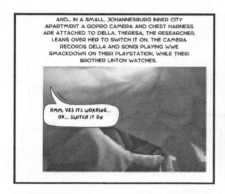

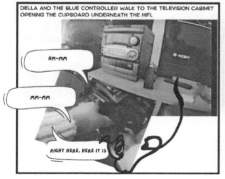
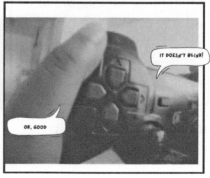

FIGURE 2.1   Postdigital story play: GoPro-girls-WWE Smackdown

DOI: 10.4324/9781003205036-2

FIGURE 2.1 (Continued)

FIGURE 2.1 (Continued)

The CTAP project's focus on children's play with technology brings to the fore children's playful relationships with the digital. This chapter sets out some of the theoretical groundwork for reconfiguring humanist notions of play, considering play from posthumanist and postdevelopmental perspectives instead. Dominant developmental perspectives consider play as an important part of children's lives and acknowledge children's agency and creativity during play. However, play and its associated agentic and creative moments are conceptualised as age- and stage-based individualised human-specific processes.

This chapter brings together play and the postdigital by considering who and what can be playful and creative. We see (child) agency and creativity as relational and distributed. We explore children's play-worlds and worlding disrupting the digital/non-digital binary. In doing so this chapter presents a theoretical and practical contribution to the concept of play and the postdigital from a posthumanist perspective.

Reconfiguring is also present in our performing-with vignettes. Here the co-created comic-vignette of World Wrestling Entertainment's 2K17 game for PlayStation, or, Smackdown, as the children refer to it, moves beyond static linguistic descriptions (Figure 2.1). This postqualitative, postdigital vignette is a de-compacted, open-edged story co-created with GoPro camera footage, Neural.Love, the AI art generator, and online graphic design software Canva. We chose a graphic novel style for this vignette, which we suspect was a contagion—caught from Della and Bongi's diary drawings animated by speech and thought bubbles and onomatopoeic sound words and by the filmic framing produced by the GoPro. An intensity of gesture, sound, and movement is present in the moments of footage, but only fragments are visible in each frame. We use the vignette to re-turn and re-configure what matters in our research as we diffract with the scholarship of others. This chapter gathers the research of others to build an argument and some momentum for our storying across subsequent chapters. In revisiting and re-reading texts through one another, we perform diffractive readings (noticing differences and patterns of difference made as they affect one another and create new possibilities for thinking) and compostings of thoughts, ideas, theories (as we turn them over and stir them up) (see Chapter 1). We sometimes follow the work of other writers to burrow deeper into places that seem to offer particularly rich opportunities for opening up and allowing in the air.

In education and research, performing a diffractive analysis involves the reading of data through texts and vice versa as well as texts and theories through one another (Murris & Bozalek, 2019b). In this meeting of difference (between the composite parts of the experience), disturbances occur. In a diffractive space, one dwells in a threshold: in-between, "both/and" (Jackson & Mazzei, 2011, p. 6). A diffractive analysis depends on the 'arts of noticing' (Tsing, 2015) realities outside the dominant discourses of schooling and childhoods. For example, in thinking with the vignette we need to be able to stay with (and trouble) our own socialised expectations: those we have of five-year-olds and our inherited notions of developmental appropriateness. Should these children be playing violent video games? How much screen time is appropriate for young children? What gender stereotypes are reinforced by this game? At the same time, we need to remain open to what emerges in the visit and the play event. Only by entering the spirit of the children's play and allowing their emotionally charged playworld to infect us, can we enact what Haraway (1997, p. 24) would call "mutated modest witnessing"—disrupting the dualist notion of the objective, dispassionate scientist.

Playing and worlding

In a book that re-turns to a project focused on play, it would be remiss of us not to invite or provoke an engagement with the concept of play. As a concept, play suggests playful engagements, and so we resist the constraints of discursive academic conventions that would demand a business-like inventory as a literature review. Avoiding the risk of producing yet another account of what has been done before, we offer an un-defining mapping of 'playing' and its possible enactments. Travelling with the disturbances of the 'post', we perform a diffractive analysis, reading play and the digital with and through one another with the help of the vignette.

It is not just young children who play

One of the powerful dominant discourses in the West assumes that play is the work of childhood. While scholarship that takes up this position, like Paley's (2009) book, *A child's work: the importance of fantasy play*, has been important in foregrounding the value of children's interests, imaginations, and inventiveness in thinking and learning, it reinforces play as human-centric and age-based. However, there is another body of work on play in education that troubles the powerful association between play and childhood, recognising its applicability to all ages (e.g., Harker, 2005; Sutton-Smith, 1966; Van Vleet & Feeney, 2015). Paley and others also stress the important role that adults perform as play companions and mentors for and with children (see also Wood, 2009; Dixon & Janks, 2019).

The vignette at the start of this chapter could simply be read as three children playing together at home. However, reading with the in/determinate boundaries of the vignette, we notice that playing

WWE Smackdown on the PlayStation connects the participant children to a broader intragenerational and international community of WWE fans and game players of adult wrestling. WWE is a media organisation and global sports entertainment company that is considered "family-friendly entertainment" and disseminated through "television programming, premium live events, digital media and publishing platforms" (World Wrestling Entertainment, 2023, company overview, para 1). Their television programming reaches over a billion homes in 25 languages. In addition, the television audience of its programme WWE Smackdown programme is not solely white, male, or American. Although WWE Smackdown's US television audience in 2022 was 55% white (Ounpraseuth & Thurston, 2022), it is the most-watched sport after cricket in India (Tamara & Nugroho, 2021). Its audience is also not age-defined but assumed to be predominantly adult with parental guidance advised. Opinion ranges among viewers as to its appropriateness for young children. Some reviews claim that earlier programming is aimed at younger audiences while later evening sections include more 'adult' content (Filucci, 2019). While the children in the study play the WWE PlayStation game offline, they are digitally connected to the related phenomena of live wrestling performances broadcast on television that inspire the digital products.

We consider WWE's world of adult professional wrestling as an example of performative play. The affective intensity, produced through both the carefully scripted and more spontaneous improvised sequences of theatrical action, is at the heart of WWE (McCreedy, 2021). The "spectacle of excess" (Barthes, 1972, p. 13) encapsulated by WWE is valued by its audiences who delight in the scripted enactment of "Suffering, Defeat and Justice" (p. 17). Through the defeat of villains, cowards, and thugs, they witness the moral victory of their heroes. These are familiar and repeated dramatic scripts that allow for moments of improvisation and skilful characterisation, coded into and then re-enacted through the WWE 2K17 PlayStation game.

We are reminded of the work of Gunilla Linqvist (1995, 2003) who revisited Vygotskyan play theories to challenge dominant cognitivist approaches to early learning that foreground learning as an individualised mental process, rather than being connected to children's shared emotions, social contexts, interests and life-worlds. Lindqvist's (1995) theorisation of the "aesthetics of play" (p. 4) in a "common playworld" (p. 10) and her research in Reggio Emilia inspired preschools in Sweden in the 1990s used drama pedagogies to create intergenerational opportunities for shared experience and the establishment of cultures of playful and affective interaction within scripted narratives.

Lindqvist's concept of 'playworld' recognises that enactments of shared cultures and narratives are capable of igniting child-adult cooperative play opportunities with imagination and creativity (Fleer, 2020). Vygotskyan theorisations recognise cultural and historical repertoires as powerfully relational and also draw our attention to the workings of thought and feeling, inside, outside, between, and among different human and non-human participants in experiential pedagogies.

These shared narrative scripts are suggestive of what Donna Haraway refers to as "inherited repertoire(s)" (Mitman, 2019, p. 18). It is not only humans who have these inherited playworlds and narrative scripts (Massumi, 2014; Haraway in Mitman, 2019). Haraway discusses this notion in relation to the play of young animals in which enjoyment and creativity produce innovation within patterns of repeated play. Haraway's and Massumi's interest in the play of animals makes important claims about how unexceptional humans are in relation to phenomena like play. Bongi and Della are involved in a digital playfight. While Della doesn't apologise when Eva Marie hits or kicks Bongi's Alexa Bliss, she does apologise to the referee avatar when Eva Marie accidentally knocks him out with a punch. "Oops, sorry Mr Ref! I did it by mistake", she says. This coheres with research that demonstrates that animals' attention to body language is the way in which playful intentions are communicated and play differentiated from real conflict (see Massumi [2014] on dogs and, Nolfo et al. [2022] on wild spotted hyenas' playfighting).

Having enquired into play as something that cannot be limited to children or to humans, and is not limited to age, it is also necessary to demythologise the inherent 'goodness' of play. Commonly accepted as a reliably 'natural' and innocent source of holistic learning and development in young children, and potentially a universally accessible enhancement of well-being for children, play needs to be recognised for its complexity and risk. Harker (2005) cautions us not to see play as liberating without considering the ways in which it can reinforce regimes of powerful discourses. Play can be both normative—working to socialise players into an imaginary norm, but can also be creative—having a liberating potential. Osgood et al. (2017) warn that neglecting to engage with the 'darker sides' of play renders these sides invisible in the debates and theorisations around children and play. Many adults are uncomfortable with the digital playworlds that are opening up to children and in some cases their avoidance and lack of knowledge cause them to be 'left behind', unable to provide guidance or support.

For us, the vignette of the WWE play event opened up the dark tropes of gender socialisation visible in the overtly sexualised costumes and choreographed poses at the start of the game when the characters make their entrances that seem to entrance Della (see also Murris et al., 2022). We note the normalisation of violent behaviour and the lack of racial diversity—Alicia Fox is the only African-American character in the two tag teams. Recognising that these elements are present does not nullify the siblings' fondness for one another, the affective draw of the sexualised costumes, or their shared pleasure in the play. As researchers, we need to sit with our readings and discomfort of a sport we know about but do not follow. In diffracting through this example of digital play a more complex dialectical reading emerges.

We recognise that the space of professional wrestling is traditionally a male-dominated and misogynistic space. In the WWE 2K17 PlayStation version of the game, there are only 25 female characters to choose from compared to 95 males. Only five are women of other ethnic or race groups (Alicia Fox, Asuka, Naomi, Sasha Banks, Tamina Snuka). However, over the last 20 years there has been a shift in how WWE promotes women and the emergence of a discourse about women's athleticism and skill rather than one only of sexualisation (Patricio, 2018). We also take note of Wood and Litherland's (2018) analysis of the influence of neoliberal feminism. They point out that despite the problems inherent in neoliberal feminism and its emphasis on the individual, it, along with fan pushback, has led to shifts in WWE's corporate policy to be more inclusive.

We also need to resist the impulse to see the digital as either dehumanising or liberatory as is common in educational discourse. Digital play is both dark and innocent. How do we think about the other members of the tag team being AI partners? What are the possibilities for playfulness and creativity? These questions contribute to our mapping of the concepts play and playing.

A pause: pondering taxonomies of play

Efforts to define and categorise play and types of play are standard fare in general play theory as well as in 'early years' educational discourse. Taxonomies of play abound in the literature, from the earliest ones defining stages of play from solitary through parallel to collaborative (e.g., Parten, 1932), to fantasy play, play with rules, play with objects etc. (Piaget cited in Sutton-Smith, 1966; Hughes, 2002), to a 'new' taxonomy of digital play (Marsh et al., 2016).

We pause for a moment to consider the concept of taxonomy and how taxonomies perform in educational research. The taxonomy has its roots in the natural sciences, as a scheme of classification for things in the world that are presumed to be autonomous entities independent of the researcher. A taxonomy indexes 'kinds' of things—to create a logically structured and fixed arrangement of reality that can be observed, measured, and recorded. While taxonomies may claim a level of neutrality: e.g., 'types of play', they are inseparable from the ontology of presence that dominates a Cartesian framing of the world as separate and 'out there' (see Chapter 3 for a discussion of scientific realism and the 'World of Objects').

In the CTAP project, one of the tools for analysis was the Learning through Play Experience Tool (LtPET). This taxonomy measures, on a hierarchical scale, the extent to which "a playful experience is agentic" and thus a meaningful learning experience for a child (Marsh et al., 2020, p. 196). The version of the tool used in the CTAP project consists of six stages of agency: Non-Play,

Passive, Responding, Exploring, Owning, and Transferring. These are measured against a set of five predetermined States of Play: Joyful, Actively Engaging, Iterative, Meaningful, and Socially Interactive (see Table 2.1).[1] The levels of agency are ranged in a developmental ordering from the top of the matrix (Non-Play) to the lowest row (Transferring) which represents the highest level or most developed stage of individual agency. The lowest row shows the desired learning through play experience across all five states of play.

The LtPET tool is generated from within the discourses of learning sciences (see Zosh et al., 2017) and is steeped in a developmental paradigm (Murris, 2022b). Staying with the LtPET tool from a postdevelopmental perspective we ask: how can the LtPET taxonomy be diffracted through in a way that allows the agency of the material and the co-productive power of collaborative engagement between and among the human and non-human to be recognised?

We appreciate that the LtPET tool sets play up as an experience that includes a range of emotions (e.g., sadness, curiosity, accomplishment, enthusiasm) rather than just reducing play to its cognitive benefits. We also value the tool's framing of the potential and possibilities offered by collaborative play experiences. However, the tool sets play experiences up as individual and human-centric. If we re-turn to the vignette it is clear that the more-than-human is central to the unfolding of the play experience. The play cannot begin without swapping to a working controller, moving a plastic garden chair sitting in front of the television away, and the pregnant pause while the children wait for the controller to communicate with the PlayStation console linked to the television to start the game.

TABLE 2.1 Learning through Play Experience Tool (LtPET) used in the CTAP project (From: Marsh et al.2020, p. 6)

State of Play	Joyful	Actively Engaging	Iterative	Meaningful	Socially Interactive
Non-Play *I am opting out of the experience*					
Passive *I am following instructions*	I am neutral about the experience	I am following the play or instructions of others	I do not know how to respond to this experience	I am doing this because I have to	I am alone or in a group not by choice
Exploring *I am considering possibilities*	I am curious about the experience	I am interested in the environment and materials	I interact with the experience	I attend to the experience	I am aware of others
Owning *I am choosing my own path*	I am enjoying the process, even if it is challenging	I am focused on the activity	I adjust my approach	I am developing my understanding	I play with others or let others approach me
Recognising *I have new insights*	I feel a sense of accomplishment	I am invested	I am deliberate about the changes I make	I show how the experience is relevant to me	I play with others collaboratively
Transferring *After the experience, I am reflecting on how this experience can influence the reality of my own life, and have confidence that it changes myself and others*	I am enthusiastic about trying this again	I have tried this again after the experience	I seek out and explore new projects	I recall the experience and use it to understand other things	I cooperate with others to initiate new play experiences

Della's body wriggles into position supported by the chair even though she speaks from within the virtual body of her avatar on screen. We argue that the meaning of the play experience described in the vignette lies in the complex and unfolding intra-actions between the children, PlayStation, remote, cables, consoles and controllers, the WWE 2K17 game, the real and virtual female wrestlers, adults, researchers, wrestling culture, a multinational corporate, computer designers and programmers, factories, workers, research design, universities, the lounge, and predictable and unpredictable porous unfoldings.

Another question that emerges about the tool (and its focus on individual measurement) is what to do with co-players, onlookers, and other less-definable play relationships. The girls' brother, Linton, participates in what could be interpreted as a more 'passive' role in the PlayStation game. In his 'non-playing' participation, he plays a productive role in the data collection as he mediates what is happening for the researchers and enthusiastically supports the players. In a postdevelopmental reading, we note the value of passivity and responsiveness in certain circumstances and therefore question the hierarchy of the stages ranked in the left-hand column of the LtPET tool. The suggestion that decision-making and autonomous control are always desirable is problematic in terms of co-play and open-ended, collaborative and negotiated exploration (with both humans and AI). Do children's intra-active agentic engagements with their environments have the potential to invite critical and caring responses towards current conditions and inspire the co-creation of different possible futures?

We appreciate the fact that children's agency is foregrounded in the LtPET tool. The assumptions underlying the tool include ideas about agency and autonomy that are at the heart of modernist progressive educational projects. These ideas about individual intention and purposeful self-directed play are closely associated with the conception of learning as teleological (directed at a goal of progress, development, and improvement). The tool sees children as agentic when children "are active in making choices about their play and have a sense of self-efficacy in relation to their play experiences" (Marsh et al., 2020, p. 196). The level of agentic engagement that is tracked is deemed to be measurable through an observation of that individual body and its performance.

However, in a posthumanist orientation, agency is not located in individual humans but distributed between and amongst intra-active bodies and participants in a meeting or encounter: in this case a play experience. As players playing this game, Della and Bongi do not pre-exist the play experience, they are produced by it. We cannot claim to know their developmental stage of ability which we would use to measure their likely response to the gaming experience. The intra-action that is the play phenomenon is a relational reality that is contingent and in/determinate. Similarly, we do not see the value of measuring each individual child against the six stages of agency as it would require a detaching of singular components from a set of close and co-constituting relationships (see Chapter 6 for more detailed reconfiguring of agency).

The same can be said for creativity. Creativity is often paired with agency as evidence of what children do when they act agentically and framed as a skill to be nurtured (see Marsh et al., 2020, pp. 6–7 and 145). While in a developmentalist orientation, creativity is expressed as an intentional enactment and cognitive skill, we propose a distributed and more-than-human creative impulse and expression. Thinking with the world (Haraway, 2016) invites a recognition of creativity as a force working across people, environments, things, energies, events etc. The play episode involving Della and Bongi is a creative engagement in which they, together with the affordances of technology and game design, create something particular. It may not be 'new' but it's a particular splice—their collaborative take on what's on offer and importantly, what draws them in and pulls them aesthetically and affectively. Through a responsive selection, they are part of a creative event. As shown in Chapter 6, their storying with this game continues iteratively in the research diaries. The diaries are fluent graphic re-turnings to the WWE game, which explore and re-script events, audience response, characters, fashion, and style.

These playful visual re-turnings raise the question about connections in-between play, art, and creativity. However, play theorists seldom include art activities in the designation of 'play', with Miller and Almon (2009) and Sakr (2017) being notable exceptions. Sakr (2017) expounds the play/creativity link to invite scholars to consider the ways that digital technology as a recent but pervasive modality co-produces different forms of play and creativity through experimentation.

Play as a worlding concept

We see play as a worlding concept. Play is an intra-active part of an emergent phenomenon. Barad (2007, p. ix) argues that emergence is iterative and reconfigured through each intra-action. Putting Barad's notion of 'phenomenon' to work here, the WWE play event is our "objective referent" (Barad, 2007, p. 309) (see Chapter 3). As such, it is a relational whole for our study. All the 'parts' (lounge, children, TV, game, PlayStation and consols, playfulness etc.) are mutually co-constitutive; they cannot be separated out and individually defined, nor presumed to have universally applicable and stable characteristics that perform in the same way in other phenomena. Harker (2005) makes a strong case for why we should not even try to define play as so many have attempted to do. We like Jones and Holmes' (2014, p. 128) proposal that play is an "ontological fugitive", defying definition. This builds on the more philosophically oriented play theorising of Sutton-Smith (1966). Play is performative and as such eludes any fixed or predictable descriptions, being always open to difference. In our agential realist account, play can be seen to come into being differently depending on the permutations and combinations of the particular "agentially intra-acting 'components'" (Barad, 2007, p. 309).

Similarly, analysing play discursively, through language, definitions, and descriptions, "ignores the fact that playing is irreducibly a *practice*. It is these lived experiential aspects of play that are constantly exceeding the confines of discourse" (Harker, 2005, p. 51). When we work to define something, the affective intensity (which is elusive, physically and emotionally embodied) is erased or overlooked.

Harker opts for the term, 'playing', a more conceptually open category than play. This move is an ontological one. It is only in the performance of playing (not play) that play/ing can be fleetingly defined in a time-space event (what we would term an intra-action). Winnicott (1971/2005) notes that the verb (playing) is more generative than the noun, drawing the attention of psychoanalysts to the *performance* of child or adult rather than to the content of play episodes (Winnicott, 1971/2005, pp. 53–54). We can say that play happens in-between being and becoming, having no discrete identity (being) other than as a characteristic of an unbounded event, the ontological difference produced through encounter (becoming). For Harker (2005, p. 58), theorising time-space as "enfolded into playing performances is vital to theorising playing". This allows us to consider the ways materiality and the physicality and emotion of bodies exceed the limits of representation captured in the early work of play theorists. So, we need to consider affective intensities—and the ways in which the affective register can become heightened. Thus, in summary, Harker (2005, pp. 57–58) notes that,

> To ignore the contingent role that objects, sounds, ideas, and socio-cultural habits have on playing performances is to ignore the specificity and complexity of these performances (or to ignore the becoming of playing).

'Play' and 'playing' in an immanent empirical sense and as a 'worlding' are not purely human concerns, nor can they be judged against an ideal set of attributes. They are 'on the ground', iteratively emergent and intra-active but also haunted by possible becomings: the real and the virtual entangled as the present unfolds in in/determinate ways. Diffractions of playfulness both as an end in itself and as a means to an end produce patterns of infinite and surprising difference.

Taking a cue from Harker (and Lindqvist), we propose 'playworlding' as a way to indicate that the players are part of a phenomenon that is playful, connected, fluid, and part of our fast-changing contemporary worlds, technology included. This brings us to a key part of the CTAP project that focuses on the digital as a component of children's play. The project's focus is an acknowledgement of the ways in which technology in all its myriad forms is already a fundamental part of play. In the following section, we consider how we understand postdigital as a concept for this book.

Postdigital is a messy concept

In the same ways as we have aimed to do in this book, many scholars currently working with postdigital thought seek not to pin down its meaning, but rather work with it in open-ended ways, in and through a range of disciplines (e.g., arts, humanities, social and natural sciences, engineering) (Jandrić et al., 2022). Jandrić et al. (2018, p. 894) argue that:

> The postdigital is hard to define; messy; unpredictable; digital and analog; technological and non-technological; biological and informational. The postdigital is both a rupture in our existing theories and their continuation.

It has been useful for us to consider the emergence of the term postdigital in the early 2000s and how, like other 'post' concepts, the postdigital looks back and forward (Tavin et al., 2021) and as a temporal reconfiguring (as discussed in Chapter 1). We recognise the postdigital then as more than a "rupture." Jandrić et al. (2018, p. 984) alert us to the idea that the postdigital is part of a flow of dis/continuity as well as a novelty—a diffraction pattern. 'Postdigital' appears to have first been used in relation to electronic music by Cascone, who described it as a glitch or computer error signalling the human in technology—or the analogue in the digital, and by Pepperell and Punt, from the visual arts, who used the metaphor of a biological membrane that both connects and divides (Cramer, 2015; Jandrić, 2022). The concepts of the glitch and membrane draw attention to the ways in which the digital and analogue intermix, and how the "technological and non-technological" and the "biological and informational" combine (Jandrić et al., 2018, p. 984). It is not helpful to think about humans as 'separate' from technology, and only connected to it if they are touching a digital device. The world we live in is replete with infrastructure and devices that power the world, with codes and programmes that are constantly collecting and recording information about us, surveilling us, managing us, navigating us, and communicating with us.

In thinking with the vignette as a postdigital moment, we follow the soundscape (see Figure 2.2 to scan the QR code). Listening carefully again, we hear the sounds of human voices in the room talking, humming, laughing; the sounds of technology connecting with bodies and wires, and the sounds emanating from the PlayStation merging with sounds in the room: the electronic opening music; the cheering crowds; the voices of the wrestling commentators; theme songs for the wrestlers' entrances; the sound of impact as avatar bodies, the mat and ropes come into contact with each other, and the distinctive noise of the bell signalling rounds. How does one distinguish what is digital and what is analogue, what is media and what is technology? The analogue morphs into

FIGURE 2.2 A postdigital soundscape: binary glitching

the digital, as biological bodies of human wrestlers are turned into information contained in bits and bytes that manifest in avatars waiting to be managed through the combination of hands, bodies, codes, and devices. The massive machinery of WWE as a professional wrestling organisation, media machine, online gaming, and music production company (with the controversial P. Diddy producing the album for WWE 2K17), reminds us of the ways in which digital technology and media are completely entangled with human life.

Thinking postdigitally moves us from conflating the digital with technology and as separate from humans. Rather the postdigital is always in flux or transition; in various shifting material-discursive entanglements with the world. This includes recognising the presence of a binary logic that sees only the dangers of over-mechanisation where technology is a "dehumanising force, set to rob individuals and communities of authentic life experience" or one where the digital is synonymous with a celebratory progress "propelling humanity towards social equality" (Knox, 2019, p. 359).

One of the ways that digital technology challenges Newtonian notions of presence, time, and space is through its invisible workings (Bluetooth, WiFi, Internet etc). We therefore find it useful to think about the power of invisibility in a postdigital world. In relation to this question, Weiser noted in 1994 that the better one's tool, the more invisible it is. When writing, one's attention needs to be on one's thoughts rather than the technology of a pen, typewriter, or keyboard. Sakr (2017, p. 14) reminds us that Heidegger's writing in *Being and Time* from 1927 recognised this move from tools being 'present-to-hand' to being 'ready-to-hand'. A good example of this is the technology of Natural User Interfaces (NUI), which improve the ease of using technology to perform thinking moves.

The touch swipe and voice recognition software features of NUIs possibly speed up this accommodation. The study of human sensory processes and their central role in meaning-making, expression, communication, and 'worlding-with' make these interface technologies possible. The intervening 'tool' or switch is not visible. The technology is activated through sound or movement.

However, assumptions about the 'invisibility' of tools can distort and misrepresent participants' contributions to visual research. In some studies, in early childhood education GoPro/wearable cameras have been assumed to *be* the 'viewpoint' of children in research (Harwood & Collier, 2019), as if they have no influence themselves. We consider this approach to be methodologically problematic. Technology works as an important material component of the research methodologies entangled with discursive framings of 'child with nature' and mutually co-productive of reality (Caton & Hackett, 2019) (see Chapter 3).

Weiser's (1994) positive appreciation for invisibility as a valuable trait of an effective tool, can be tempered with posthumanist and decolonial 'noticings' of the workings of technology. The invisibility and increasingly ubiquitous presence of digital technology in governing socio-technical infrastructure, geopolitics, and markets as well as its ongoing contribution to anthropogenic global degradation is part of what constitutes the postdigital (Cramer, 2015; Knox, 2019; Kuhn et al., 2023). Knox (2019) raises ethical concerns about the invisibility of the environmentally destructive and violently exploitative labour practices currently shielding platform capitalism from any accountability. Children (and the CTAP researchers), as consumers of digital products, are part of the postdigital community implicated in the extractive and exploitative mechanisms of late capitalist production. Revisiting the vignette, we diffract with the notion of postdigital consumption to produce another figuration of the vignette to foreground the materiality of technology (Figure 2.3).

Along with a decolonial noticing is a posthumanist undoing of the inside/outside binary that recognises the labour and environmental implications of digital technology production. Indeed, according to Qiu (cited in Knox, 2019), the light and effortless technologies of the digital age and the equally accessible and connected corners of the world are possible thanks only to the violent, exploitative, and destructive technologies employed in the production of the devices and systems that keep them running. By no means post-industrial, the conditions under which mobile phones and other technological devices, like the ones we used to collect and co-create data, are produced constitute a version of contemporary slavery. The work involved in component manufacture, assembling, polishing, packing, and distributing is lowly paid and part of a massive exploitative machine, predominantly based

FIGURE 2.3   Postdigital story play: entangling-GoPro-PlayStation-Fingers Controller-Cables

in China, where capitalist efficiencies recruit the legacies of communist centralist conformity and control. Sony's PlayStations are made in China. Data from 2022 indicates that over 563.2 million PlayStation consoles have been sold since 1994. For example, 87.4 million are PlayStation 3s, with 999 million games being sold for this model (Susic, 2023).

Taking the obvious next step in a posthumanist tracing of the material-discursive reality that is digital technology, leads us to noticing the relations of responsibility and response-ability as researchers. We pay attention to the international extraction and trade in the key minerals required in its manufacture. Poor countries are effectively held in patterns of war and ungovernability due to the competitive and coercive methods used by large multinational corporations with economies multiple times the size of their national GDP. In the early 2000s, this came to be known as the PlayStation Wars. Examples of mining of rare-earth metals that are used for hardware are tantalum, tin, tungsten, gold (3TGs), and cobalt. Tantalum capacitors are used to build PlayStations. Highly sought after by the IT industry, they are mined in several African countries including DRC, Rwanda, Nigeria, Ethiopia, and Mozambique. In the DRC, in particular, they are mined under conditions of non-existent human or environmental rights management by artisanal groups under conditions of conflict, and the commodities are often undeclared and smuggled. Although companies have been required to report back on their supply chains since 2014, Sony traditionally has had a poor record. Sony's report for the 2021 financial year indicates that 84 of its 339 Smelters or Refineries are non-compliant, the location of 47 is unknown as well as the information about where 3TGs are sourced from (Sony, 2022). These unmonitored extraction processes in various parts of the world cause extensive ecological damage.

It is important then to acknowledge that play is entangled with/ in the world as we consider what matters in postdigital play.

Postdigital play

When we watch and re-watch the GoPro recording of the WWE play event, different parts of its narrative gain importance. We notice the theatrical entrances that the four avatars make before the match begins. As each avatar swaggers and struts into the ring, playing to the crowd, the GoPro camera, resting in its harness on Della's chest, moves almost imperceptibly up and down in time to even breaths. In contrast to the spectacle unfolding on the television screen, arms rest on the chair, the controller sits in Della's lap, legs crossed quietly at the ankles, the body transfixed. Della has a fleeting conversation with Theresa about Alexa Bliss's gloves that look like handbones, but mostly the conversation flows around Della and her other on-screen self. The height and position of this small girl-body-Go-Pro cut the television screen in half in the video recording creating a tangle of legs: avatars from the waist down strut their 'fleshy' legs above girl-legs clad in pink stripey leggings.

We read this as an example of postdigital play. It is an obvious example of the way in which the digital is a pervasive part of everyday life. In this case, the pervasiveness is realised in the material objects that enable this kind of digital play, but it also reveals the politics of the digital that raises questions about access and digital inequality. While these children are playing with products from two multinational brands, they do not have the latest PlayStation model, the most current version of WWE Smackdown, nor does their family have the financial means to pay for the data or infrastructure costs to play online. A decolonial orientation to the postdigital reminds us that the material conditions instantiated by commercial interests and available technological infrastructure are two key factors in the production and perpetuation of inequality across the global "media worlds" of children in different geographical locations (Horst & gaspard, 2020, p. 39).

While there is a substantial body of work on children's digital play, the postdigital reconfigures digital play by considering how "diverse sets of bodies, sensations, devices and materials are recruited into the situation and experience of play" (Apperley et al., 2017, p. 203). This disrupts binary thinking that sees play from the perspective of a value judgement (Harker, 2005). It unsettles developmental understandings of digital play that see it as something harmful or dangerous for children's social and cognitive development as compared to 'normal' play. In many early childhood settings the use of digital technologies has been discouraged because it is seen as too abstract for children to manage, not developmentally appropriate and as stripping children of a 'natural' childhood (Edwards, 2023). However, the development of NUIs and specific programming for children that develops abstract thinking and problem-solving challenges this view. This response is also affected by narrow conceptions of child. Burnett and Merchant (2020, p. 12) note that the view of child as innocent manifests as "digital innocence" where children need to be protected from technology. They suggest that this belief has more to do with limiting children's participation than with maintaining their 'innocence'.

An example of a more participatory approach to children and technology comes from the global south. The African Storybook

Project (www.africanstorybook.org) has created an in-house app that can be used both online and offline to promote the sharing, creation, and collaboration of stories outside of any platform capitalist system. It effectively excludes toy and game marketing corporations, even though it is dependent on smartphone producers.

Postdigital play disrupts the online/offline, digital/non-digital, human/machine binaries. For many young people, the distinction between online and offline practices is superfluous (Collier & Perry, 2023), as the WWE Smackdown playscapes show. Apperley et al.'s (2017) notion of the 'aesthetics of recruitment' illustrates how postdigital play is less about the devices (e.g., computers and consoles) but focuses rather on the "processes and practices of interfacing that negotiate multiple and hybrid bodies, devices and objects" (Apperley et al., 2017, p. 210). We think about the multiple elements that become part of the play experience during the WWE play event. However, what and who is recruited is unpredictable and relations are asymmetrical and contingent. The aesthetics of recruitment are related to how game designs affect the play experience and our capacity to respond. The capacity of individuals and things to respond opens up space for creative acts. We know that children's play events exceed and confound expectations of how designers (and teachers) prescribe the use of games and devices (Nansen et al., 2019; Burnett & Merchant, 2020).

The intentional use of 'interfacing' rather than 'interface' by Apperley et al. (2017) is important and speaks to the messiness of the postdigital. They explain that interfaces are not stable delineations between 'real' space that contains players and devices and 'virtual' space presented on a screen. The "interfaces arise and decompose in a more dynamic fashion as different bodies, sensations, devices and objects come into, and fall out of relations"

(Apperley et al., 2017, p. 207). Coherent with our use of the Baradian term, 'phenomenon', this notion of interfacing is relational and ontological (see Chapter 3).

The blue controller Della held in Figure 2.1 was recruited into the play event and then fell out of it as she used a black controller. Linton is a part of the entanglement, his body responds sensorially as it begins to dance when Alexa Bliss's entrance music begins and he's drawn to the avatars on the screen as he flits across the room, with tactile knowledge that connects to the television screen. The GoPro is also entangled in the play event: a playful technology deployed as a research instrument that comes into relation with other bodies and things, its presence altering ways of knowing and doing for Della, child-turned cyborg, and for us as researchers. This device's "playful behaviour is continuous with, yet also exceeds the digital through conditions that are technical, historical, aesthetic and affective" (Apperley et al., 2017, pp. 204–205). It has called to us to play with the recording, reconfiguring the play event transmodally in Figure 2.1 as we think with the postdigital.

In the same way, WWE Smackdown and the PlayStation "*act on and with* the social world" (Burnett & Merchant, 2020, p. 23 original italics) in this small Johannesburg apartment as the affective and aesthetic pull of avatars' costumes are re-assembled as part of an ongoing playworlding that manifests in drawings in research diaries (see Chapter 6). We recognise that this playworlding co-constitutes itself with the research diaries as part of the postdigital play phenomenon. The notion of postdigital play removes the assumption that a physical technological device marks the digital (Cramer, 2015).

We note that there is a growing body of work around connected play (Stevenson, 2021) that focuses on 'smart toys' with electronic components that connect to other devices and/or the Internet. Marsh's (2017) study of Amy's play is one example. Amy's connected play focuses on Furby Boom! and Paw Patrol toys that are networked toy/robot/app systems. The child plays with these, together with an iPad on which the related apps play out. Amy's body, movements, and narrative are strong co-creating elements of the play phenomenon together with the different toys, computer components embedded inside them, and the iPad.

However, the edges of the vignette about Amy's play require some stretching and fraying. Amy and her toy are part of a reality that extends beyond her physical playspace. A 'slowing down' (see Chapter 1) to notice the complexities and ethically entangled worldings-with allows for a re-configuring of the story. Marsh's study draws attention only to the connections between the participants (both human and non-human) and their *digitally* connected counterparts as though in a sealed 'digital' container. Our use of the postdigital requires noticing the entanglement of play-worlding with realities of justice and the inseparability of issues of play and the relations between north and south, 'developed' and 'under-developed'. The home-space intra-actions involving child, toy, Internet, imagination, and fur are always already contaminated and entangled with other strongly related realities—like those of child soldiers in the DRC and the mining of 3TGs. These are connections and relations of response-ability (Barad, 2007).

The 'postdigital' as a term may make this noticing appear to be a newly relevant concern since the coming of the digital age, but it is in fact an ontological point being made here, not a historical one. Colonial and inherited forms of schooling have created the spaces and relationships we assume to be constructive of the benign educational project we have bought into, but they are always part of the global systems that created it. Ontologically, the Furby is not separate from the warzone, nor is the researcher and the academic advantage gained from the study.

Pettersen et al. (2022) make an important contribution to research into postdigital play by creating an ethnographic socio-material 'vignette' of postdigital play that does not include the physical presence of a networked or connected toy but shows the affordances of the digital and its hauntings for play and playing. In Pettersen et al.'s (2022) example, play re-emerges in different forms of collaboration in the preschool space, as the children play Minecraft with blocks. In Africa, with high data costs and families with low incomes, connected play is less of a feature. In these digitally less-connected contexts, children take opportunities to connect and play on smart devices when they arise. Understanding children's capacity to respond in such contexts that are not well resourced, middle class, global north is part of a decolonial orientation and an important part of the conversation about digital play.

An open-ended un/con/clusion

In this chapter, we think-with postdigital play as a boundaryless intra-action of old and new technologies, senses, bodies, thoughts, and ongoing and re-turning realities. An agential realist 'thinking-with' moves away from the human or child-centred and developmental notions of play that we take into the following chapters. In the next chapter, in particular, a vignette is 'played with' to reveal the differences that an agential realist 'intra-pretation' can make.

Playing and playworlding are phenomena that are always differently made up of co-constituting parts and are inseparably entangled with issues of justice. We end this chapter by considering play, the digital and the postdigital, as part of educational research. Knox (2019) notes that education research and particularly research focussing on pedagogy has so far been chiefly concerned with what has been conceptualised as the 'inner' aspects of human learning and the relationships between human participants, teachers, learners, and communities. Digital technology and e-learning have been considered as 'outer'. These areas of theory and practice have formed discrete and distinctive areas of scholarship and institutional departments outside of the central concerns of the educational project.

Despite the seemingly negative impact of the highly competitive marketing strategies employed in the digital gaming industry where young children are concerned, there is still space for creative alternatives to predatory corporate products to operate in the digital space.

Technology needs to be recognised as a force that is shaping the central concerns of education (Knox, 2019, p. 316). It can no longer occupy a marginal space in early years educational research or theorisation where most of our work is focused.

Note

1 This table has since been revised by the LEGO Foundation. Non-Play has been removed as a state of agency. See https://learningthrough-play.com/learning-through-play-experience-tool for August 2020 version. We use this version because it was used to analyse the CTAP data.

3

PLAYING WITH LENSES

from 'Object', to 'Subject', to 'Phenomenon'

In many research projects, little attention is paid to the materiality of the devices that are used to 'collect' data. They are often invisible, a means to an end in what eventually comes to be 'research data'. Although the Children, Technology and Play (CTAP) project observed children and their families' digital play practices, the technology we used to do this was not an explicit focus. The devices asserted themselves during and after the project raising questions and challenges for us. In this chapter we return to two of these devices, smartphone cameras and GoPros, to think differently with them.

For us, digital technology is not simply the *medium* (a neutral research instrument) that records what happens as a matter of fact 'in' space and time and creates 'data'. As we have seen in Chapter 1, 'post' approaches reconfigure research as *non-representational*. In the context of educational research, this means that the recording devices we use in research are *not* understood as accurately representing a world out there—a slice of reality from a World of Objects that is ontologically independent from the human holding

DOI: 10.4324/9781003205036-3

the camera or the materiality of the camera (Murris & Menning, 2019). Digital devices play a central and agential role in the co-creation of particular data. Humans and more-than-human are always entangled phenomena in our choice of technical apparatuses.

In playing with lenses as a concept that includes the human 'eye', the eye of the camera (in this case, the smartphone and GoPro cameras), and theoretical lenses, we show how they work to include and exclude in educational research. In noticing 'what else' is going on, education research globally can move away from the dominant role of human vision in knowing and seeing (see Murris & Peers, 2022) and deciding what is real in research and what counts as 'objective' or 'subjective' knowledge. In this chapter, troubling humancentrism involves exploring the implications of how adult humans construct child subjectivity through the digital. In fact, ironically, the analysis amplifies the role of the human in research and by doing so opens up posthumanist possibilities for other ways of knowing and be(com)ing at any age.

This chapter makes us think differently in theory *and* practice about knowledge and educational relationality (between Adult humans and child humans, researchers and research participants, as well as between humans and the more-than-human). In doing so it 'cracks the lens' between culture and nature that shapes asymmetrical research relations and decolonises play (see Chapters 1 and 2).

The aim of this chapter is threefold. First, we focus our literal and metaphorical lenses on two of the participant children and show the importance of staying with *the specificity* of vignettes. As stated in Chapter 1, unlike case studies which are considered to be bounded, our posthuman vignettes have porous boundaries.

By telling a story of Eshal and Henry, we disrupt familiar understandings of causality, as well as times and places preceding one another and producing an effect (Barad, 2007, 2012). In our storying, we play with, and subvert, the 'correct' ordering of time and space with digital devices as the central characters. Staying with each story in their specificity gives insight into *differences*— differences that matter not only politically and ethically, but also epistemologically and ontologically. One of the key differences that matter is the location of the school these children[1] attend and where these children live.

The second aim of the chapter is to illustrate our take on postdigital play in Chapter 2 and disrupt the universality and innocence of digital devices in educational research. Using a geopolitical lens, we draw attention to the complexity of researching children's digital play practices, especially the introduction of the GoPro camera and the dilemmas it brought into focus (Murris & Peers, 2022). In our re-turning to the CTAP data we show the *non-innocence* of the digital technologies humans use and how technologies use 'us' human animals discursively.

The third aim of this chapter is to reconfigure the notion of (digital) play by focusing our lenses not on *objects* (e.g., camera, child, videoclip), nor on *subjects* (e.g., child as co-researcher, adult researcher). Instead, a postqualitative lens shifts our adult human gaze to how visual data can be analysed as *phenomena*. We do this through a carefully staged analysis of a video clip 'of' Henry, first through the human lens of *child-as-object*, secondly as *child-as-subject*, and finally as *child-as-phenomenon* in the final part of the chapter. Diffracting visual data through one another affects how our eyes are literally in touch with still images and moving data clips. We show how the methodology of temporal diffraction ('hauntology') opens up affirmative decolonising possibilities to engage with what is in/visible in data.

Before exploring these three aims we discuss our approach to research as one that draws on a notion of embodied feminist objectivity to illustrate the ways in which research lenses are never innocent.

Embodied feminist objectivity and non-innocent lenses

In this chapter, we work with a reconfigured notion of *objectivity*, by paying attention to *differences* in the stories the vignettes tell, rather than the common practice in educational science of foregrounding what they have *in common*. Finding similarities is a common feature of qualitative data analysis (e.g., enabled by using software) and acknowledging the *subjectivity* of the researchers is seen as an asset, rather than a shortcoming. In contrast, and inspired by Karen Barad's agential realism (2007, 2017a,b), this chapter disrupts how we tend to think in a binary way about objectivity in education research, that is, as something *in opposition to subjectivity*. Profoundly influenced by Donna Haraway who argues that one's own situatedness as a researcher is already part of the 'data' that is produced, agential realism challenges the scientific realist objectivist 'view from *nowhere*', Haraway writes:

> There is no unmediated photograph or passive camera obscura in scientific accounts of bodies and machines; there are only highly specific visual possibilities, each with a wonderfully detailed, active, partial way of organizing worlds ... Understanding how these visual systems work, technically, socially, and psychically, ought to be a way of embodying feminist objectivity.
>
> *(Haraway, 1988, p. 583)*

Agential realism gives us a technology of embodiment (Barad, 1996), a "feminist objectivity." Intricately connected to the notion of objective knowledge, the materiality of the body always implies 'a view from *somewhere*'. Paying attention to *material realities* means incorporating material-discursive factors (including age, gender, race, sexuality, religion, and nationality, as well as class) but also technoscientific and natural factors. Also, what constitutes the 'natural' or the 'cultural' is part of the investigation. This is because these notions are always already implied in the reconfiguration of the material relations of the world. We argue that by paying attention to the *non-innocent use of lenses* and how the technology worked with/in the data in research allows us to do more justice to the material-discursive complexity of these children's lives.

Postqualitative research does not to do away with qualitative research, but works differently with data and opens up new perspectives of what counts as data. As Mirka Koro-Ljungberg and colleagues point out, data is not just "raw," "brute," "inert," "passive," "simple," "concrete," and "lifeless," waiting to be "collected," "extracted," and "coded," in order to be analysed, interpreted, theorised, or used as evidence, but

> something must always be done to them to render them fit for human consumption ... Data are implicated in deep questions about the boundaries, or lack thereof, between the word and the world, between reality and representation, between nature and culture.
>
> *(Koro-Ljungberg et al., 2018, pp. 806–807)*

This 'doing to data' includes the possibility for us as researchers and transcribers to repeatedly play back the recordings and experience them differently. These postdigital affordances offer unique material-discursive opportunities to explore "in detail the effects of specific ways of seeing with a camera" (Mengis et al., 2016, p. 4). Similarly, Gilles Deleuze argues that images can do some important work to disrupt "dominant modes of perception" (Cole & Bradley, 2016, p. 12). In Claire Colebrook's (2002, p. 29) reading of Deleuze, technology allows "a reception of data that is not located in a subject". It liberates "the sequencing of images from any single observer" to "the presentation of 'any point what-ever'" (2002, p. 31).

The digital camera is not innocent, but always political in the sense that lenses do not simply reproduce and represent (Cole & Bradley, 2016, p. 7). Of course, especially in education, the humanities and the social sciences, many researchers acknowl-edge the fact that video recordings as popular research instru-ments are open for epistemic contestation, interpretation, and different subjective or intersubjective analyses (Knoblauch & Schnettler, 2012), but almost without exception a particular west-ern ontology remains intact (Jewitt, 2012). Indeed, many scientists do not realise how practices of representing are in and by them-selves *performative* and don't *model* the world-as-it-is (Murris & Menning, 2019). Sylvia Kind (2013) argues for the need to actively disrupt the common assumption that cameras simply objectively record movements and represent the real world—a disruption essential to postcolonial research. Video- and sound-recording devices are not objective instruments that record how things *are* in the world independent from human interventions but are mate-rially implicated in the production of new knowledge and mobi-lise new social and cultural relations (de Freitas, 2016, p. 554). Even those committed to the poststructuralist dismantling of the humanist subject find it extremely difficult to "escape the 'I'" (St. Pierre, 2011, p. 620).

Re-turning to one pack of crayons, two children, and two GoPros

Sitting with the shared stories around the table in Scarborough[2] we re-member the families and the fieldwork. Scrolling through the data our gaze is held by the finer details in this particular photograph (Figure 3.1) taken during a school visit at the end of the project.

At first glance, the configuration of books, crayons, hands, and bodies around a table is unsurprising in a classroom setting. In this moment, the photograph becomes more than an archived, labelled image in a digital folder of classroom observations. It interrupts our stories. The crayons, slightly hidden under a book, push another story into view.

Two names are written on a label on the crayon packaging: Eshal and Henry.[3] These crayons belong to both children and point to shared histories of drawing, learning, and making together. The page of a book from the local library is turned by Eshal's fingers as she tells Henry and others about her interest in oceans and land. As we stay with the peeking crayons, they speak of the interwoven playworlds of these children who are more than classmates, they are friends.

In this moment, the crayons draw out a memory of a home visit Joanne made to Eshal's home. Eshal turned the tables on Joanne, resisting being an interviewee, and asking penetrating questions about the GoPro cameras and how they were being

FIGURE 3.1   Relating through crayons

allocated to children (Figure 3.2). "Eshal asked me about the GoPros", Joanne says. We pause at the tone of her voice. "I remember feeling the discomfort of two different plans for the GoPro with Eshal and Henry". She continues, "One, that we would leave the GoPro camera at Eshal's house but we'd only take it with us for Henry's home visits". The crayons linger as Chanique and Joanne scroll through transcripts. Eshal's presence fills the room. We hear Joanne being caught off guard, the change in her tone, in her pauses, as she sidesteps Eshal's politely phrased persistence:

FIGURE 3.2 The lens on research

> *Eshal:* **Do you have lots of GoPros? For all of the children?**
>
> *Joanne:* No, so…
>
> *Eshal:* **How many do you have?**
>
> *Joanne:* We don't have GoPros for everyone. We only have GoPros for, um, the children who were able to use the GoPro, or if we were going to be visiting them for long enough.
>
> *Eshal:* **How many GoPros do you have?**
>
> *Joanne:* I don't know, I think there were eleven children, I think there's probably about six families … Ja.

One in Joburg. So, some children are using the
GoPro, some people are using their phones. Uhh,
some of them use the GoPro when we visit them.

Eshal: **So, do you have for Henry? Henry told me he has
a GoPro.**

Joanne: Yes, so, when we go to Henry... [We take the
GroPro to him for use during the home visit only]

Eshal: [interrupts] ... Wednesday, and then another
Wednesday.

Joanne: Yes, that's right.

Eshal: He says so. Then he says 'Miss Peers is coming'
[Laughs].

A memory of 'another Wednesday' is sparked as someone talks
about the final home visit. Henry had been unable to attend
school that day because service delivery protests had taken place
and had made it too dangerous for him to walk to school.

FIGURE 3.3   Researching response-abilities: sticking with protest,
smells, fears, noise, and home visits

The two children, Eshal and Henry, whose stories converge in this vignette, attend the same school which is located at the edge of Vrygrond. Henry lives in Vrygrond. Eshal lives two kilometres walking distance away from Henry in the suburb of Muizenberg which was a 'white' suburb during Apartheid.

A geopolitical reading of Vrygrond performs a complex hauntology. Historically this area has hosted seasonal fishing communities over hundreds of years that predate the colonisation of the Cape. The informal houses of Vrygrond were erected by Trek fishermen, fishermen who fish using large nets which are pulled onto the shore. The legend exists that the land was named Vrygrond, 'free ground' when it was 'gifted' to the local community by an Italian nobleman. The community is also entangled in colonial whaling practices, where communities were able to subsist on whale carcasses that washed ashore after the whaling boats had removed their blubber and then cast them off.

In recent years, Vrygrond has been shaped by the laws of segregation and forced removals of the Apartheid government (see Act 36 of the Group Areas Act of 1966) on the grounds of race. Vrygrond became a designated 'township' for people racially classified as 'black' or 'coloured'. Townships were areas which were close enough to service areas that had been designated for white people. The legacy of this inequitable resourcing, segregation, and racial violence continues as residents continue to occupy land illegally in order to access employment. Residents' houses and shacks don't comply with official planning and building regulations.

Crowther's (2021, pp. 98–100) research tells a story of ongoing geopolitical hauntologies of Vrygrond. She amplifies the presence of economic hardship, gang violence, housing backlogs, high crime levels, fatal diseases, and migrancy that are entangled with/

in the area. Huge income disparity, deep inequalities, high unem-
ployment, lack of safe public transportation, and gender violence
pose profound challenges to doing research in Vrygrond.

But living closely together in Vrygrond, with easy access to other
children who also like to play games, brings other affordances and
a sense of community that the materiality and infrastructure of middle-class houses in residential areas make difficult to build. South
African anthropologist Fiona Ross (2005, p. 632) shares a story of
how an elder moving on from his shack to take up residence in
an *'ordentlik'* (Afrikaans for 'decent') government house involves
the loss of the stories routinely told around the communal water
tap. Without romanticising Vrygrond, we also need to resist deficit
descriptions and do justice to its material-discursive affordances as
a *place*. We also need to be realistic about the risks involved in
doing research with/in these communities and what this means for
us in terms of response-ability.

Response-ability as articulated by Barad in an interview, is "a
matter of inviting, welcoming, and enabling the response of the
Other. That is, what is at issue in response-ability—the ability to
respond" (Kleinman & Barad, 2012, p. 81). We have playfully diffracted images through one another at the end of the vignette
(Figure 3.3) to articulate the sticky affect of the sunny sky, traffic
lights, smells, smoke, fears, GoPro, car side mirror, and the noise
of the protest which are wrapped up in the making of the sackball
during that home visit. We include this image to make it possible
for the land to respond as part of this vignette.

What would a different sense of 'account-ability' and 'response-
ability' bring about? The notion of response-ability also involves
paying renewed attention to the research design, to interview
questions asked during the home visit, and providing certain

technologies like the GoPro cameras to measure play. As a research team, we had discussed the problem of the GoPro and made decisions about how to manage it. In Eshal's case, the GoPro would stay in her home, but this wasn't the case with Henry. However, we had decided that, as researchers, we needed to take responsibility for possibly exposing Henry and his family to theft and violence and therefore the most ethical decision was to only use the GoPro on our home visits and not to leave it with the family. The cost of one GoPro is approximately equivalent to one month's salary of 25% of people living in the Western Cape[4].

We did not anticipate that our young participants would notice or question our research practices. By asking about the inconsistent use of our research tools, Eshal shifts the asymmetrical power relations between researcher and participant (Adult and child). In presuming that the two children could be treated differently as discrete and separate units within the research design, we had made an error of judgement, excluding the participants from important decisions relating to the enactment of our research methodology. The close and empathetic friendship between the two children, who share a table, a pack of crayons, a learning collaboration in the classroom, and daily conversation makes the dilemma starkly apparent.

It is significant that this experience with Eshal resurfaced around the table at Scarborough (Figure 1.2). We recognise that making a 'unilateral' decision about what is 'good for one child and what is good for another' in this instance, is a colonial move. It is misplaced to assume that Henry and his family do not understand the dangers of the place they live in and cannot be included in the deliberations.

Staying with the vignette and dwelling in the specificity of the entangled stories of Henry and Eshal exposes the non-innocence of the lenses we use as research instruments. Reading with crayons, Eshal and the GoPros turn the lens onto our research practices (Figure 3.3) making us re-turn to our decisions. The ethical decisions about when and where and how to use or not use expensive technologies are complex and entangled with the land. Making a universal decision that children living in poor, unsafe, or risky circumstances do not get access to something like a GoPro camera denies them access to the devices and experiences thus perpetuating another set of inequalities. It is important to stay with the trouble.

In the next section, the troublesome GoPro travels with Joanne and Henry in the second vignette as we consider how visual data can be analysed as a phenomenon rather than focusing on objects or subjects as is common practice in research.

From Object to Subject to Phenomena: Slowing down Henry

During the second home visit, Henry's father talked about his son's love of soccer. He shared how balls are made in the community using items like plastic bags, paper, and tape. The balls are often referred to as sackballs. For members of these communities, the ball is not a plastic object or just any soccer ball. It becomes a sackball when its softness and flexibility make soccer something different on the dusty, rough, and uneven ground of the lanes and streets in Vrygrond.

Newspaper, plastic bags, and tape arrive in a bag with researchers on the afternoon of the final visit with Henry and his parents. These materials are going to be transformed into a sackball. The researchers have no idea how to make one. The ball-making takes place outside the front door of his house in between the corrugated zinc sheet-lined lanes. Henry's sticky taping hands move skilfully, directed by memories and movements of previous sack-ball-making. These hands lead the storying as he educates the researchers (Figure 3.4).

The tape starts to run out. Between the movements of sticky fingers and tape, Henry and his mother talk to each other in Chichewa (see Chapter 4). Then Henry springs into action, ready to run to the shops to buy more tape. The GoPro camera comes along for the trip. Legs run through the maze of breeze block and zinc lanes, hands exchange money, fingers grasp tape, and the walk back commences. Walking behind Henry, Joanne's voice asks how much the tape costs. The time-lapse button catches Joanne's finger, filming the return trip home in slow motion ...

[Scan the QR code in Figure 3.5 to watch the rest of the vignette.]

It is difficult to resist pitying Henry for not having 'the real thing', a 'genuine' soccer ball. It is indeed terribly difficult to move away from

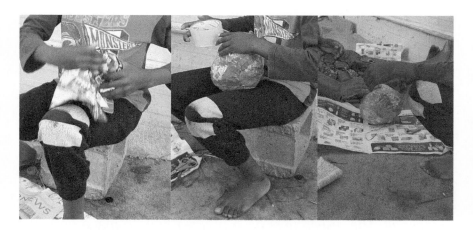

FIGURE 3.4   Sackball making

deficit interpretations and discourses that position black children living in poverty as 'less-than'. It requires considerable *unlearning* because the dominant western positioning of children as vulnerable, innocent, and ignorant is deeply engrained (Murris, 2016). We are interested in the role technology plays in affirming and helping sediment these developmental beliefs about what children lack. The lenses we use and that use us, profoundly inform our judgements about child and child agency in digital play. We ask: how can choreographing the digital lenses we use be helpful in raising awareness of *how we are used by lenses*—our own eyes as well as the technologies at our disposal?

During our conversations and the materiality of the writing process itself, the decolonising affordances of the postdigital emerged. By troubling the very distinction between human and more-than-human lenses, 'inhuman'[5] lenses can do their decolonising work. Yet, we are not proposing that playing with digital lenses in research holds the promise of going *beyond* binaries (as if we could) but

FIGURE 3.5   Slowing down Henry: a diffractive reading of the data

about questioning what differentially constitutes these binaries. How do the binaries work to include and exclude, and why does that matter especially for education research?

As a helpful way of enquiring into these questions, we turn to the moment that Henry comes back from the shops (scan the QR code in Figure 3.5). Thinking-with this time-lapsed video clip, we let ourselves be affected by Henry and his movements as he is returning with the sticky tape. The video was not deliberately choreographed afterwards, although the decision to stop the video at that point (with Henry's arms stretched high up) is a deliberate intra-vention, which we theorise as the text below unfolds.

We think with this video clip to continue by exploring in more detail how different lenses in research can bring about different subjectivities and therefore influence how we analyse digital play. First, we focus our analysis on research that assumes a world that consists of *Objects*. For example, the child-as-Object, but also the camera (Smartphone and GoPro) and the videoclip itself. Secondly, we then ontologically shift to a world of human *Subjects* (e.g., child as co-researcher, adult researcher). Thirdly, we complete this section by shifting our Adult human gaze to how human and more-than-human lenses can be analysed as *Phenomena*. Of particular importance for this chapter is how and why we use digital lenses as research instruments and how they work as part of how the world worlds itself.

For example, in Figure 3.2 we can see with our human lenses (eyes) Eshal wearing a GoPro on her chest. The reason for using the digital camera lens in this way is that as part of CTAP's socio-constructivist research design, the eye of the GoPro assists the human researcher in co-creating data from Eshal's unique subjective perspective and that the digital lens gives her 'a voice'. A researcher might 'choose' (assuming one does that) the paradigm that shapes her research design and the technology she adopts as part of that (see Table 3.1). In our case, we worked within the project's socio-constructivist research paradigm. How the other paradigms work to theorise different uses of digital devices unfolds below. An essential part of the reading of this section is *accessing the QR code and watching the video clip several times when reading each 'world' below*: the **World of Objects** (quantitative research), **Subjects** (qualitative research) and **Phenomena** (post-qualitative research).

To express the idea that paradigms are not neat boxes or fixed categories, but can be playfully diffracted through one another (Kuby, 2021), Table 3.1 has no lines separating the paradigms. Our theoretical lenses are apparatuses that perform particular research practices for which we are response-able as researchers. They assume world views and philosophies of life. These in turn inform how the concepts we use perform and the meanings we bring to concepts such as 'self', 'causality', 'intentionality', 'will', 'play', and many more in research. Each paradigm in Table 3.1 is intra-cately connected to these 'worlds', The World of Objects with the scientific realism paradigm, the World of Subjects with the constructionist and socio-constructivist paradigm, and the World of Phenomena with the posthumanist and agential realist paradigm. Our focus is on the implications of these different lenses for how differences are made and unmade in digital play research; what is (made) invisible and erased but leaves sticky traces (e.g., colonisation).

The World of Objects

Each theory assumes a particular ordering of the world—a particular ontology (**onto** means 'being'). The use of the human lens—the

TABLE 3.1 Digital lenses as research instruments in different research paradigms

	Scientific Realism	Constructionism Social-constructivism	Agential Realism Posthumanism
		Poststructuralism	
Digital technology as research instrument	The eye of the camera represents nature/the world-as-it-is and what as a matter of fact happened in space and time ('closed event')	The eye of the camera extends the human eye and assists the human to (co) create knowledge about other humans and the world.	Aesthetic manipulation of visual data reconfigures what counts as data (its ontology, epistemology, and ethics)
	More objective than the eye of the human	Acknowledging human's inherent subjectivity in creating and reading data that as such exists separately from the researcher	
	Captures 'slices' of the past, ready for analysis	Decolonises by affirming the importance of identity (assumes Newtonian notions of space and time)	Decolonises by disrupting the binary logic of identity (assumes spacetime dis/continuities of quantum physics)

eye—has been dominant since Ancient Greek philosophy and science. Vision, visibility, and ocular metaphors (Lakoff & Johnson, 1980) structure what humans have decided as real and counts as truth and reliable knowledge (a metaphysics of 'presence'). See, for example, Descartes' (1968) proposition that knowledge should be 'clear and distinct'. For the human eye, the world consists of things, of objects as it scans the world from a particular human scale. Assuming a World of Objects (including people as objects) is at the heart of a scientific view of the (real) world. From the perspective of scientific realism, a child is an object that can be monitored, observed, and measured objectively through quantitative measures. Child is still developing and in the process of becoming an Adult.

Using this (normative) lens as we access the QR code in Figure 3.5, we 'see' Henry returning from the shop followed by an adult who is guiding him as he buys from the store. The digital lens expresses this 'natural' hierarchy between child and adult by filming from adult height.

Also, for the scientific realist, the eye of the camera is understood as more objective than the eye of the human. The GoPro captures 'slices' of the past, ready for analysis and there is only one accurate way of describing what happened in the past. Protagonists of this philosophical position would argue that 'normally speaking' such film clips represent the event in the world-as-it-is and as what happened in space and time as a 'closed event'. The past cannot be changed. Of course, in this particular case, the video was slowed down by accident. From the child-as-Object perspective, this would be seen as very unfortunate because it now *distorts* what in reality did not happen as a matter of fact. Thus, the video no longer represents reality accurately. If the clip had been at 'normal' speed, it would have been more reliable as a *representation* (see also Chapter 1).[6] The objectivity provided for by the correct use of technology would enable researchers to evaluate the child's actions against prescribed benchmarks, standards, and norms. The child-as-Object is the child as understood through the lens and study of cognitive psychology.

For scientific realists, the very fact of the lens recording the event does not change or influence the event itself. The camera has no agency; instead, agency is located *in* the human using the camera. Joanne used the GoPro to collect data when she, Luiza, and Heloisa were interviewing Henry at his home. Part of the interview was the making of the sack ball and following Henry to the shops. In the World of Objects, Henry is the object of observation and the object that observes (the GoPro) doesn't change the event itself. As part of this paradigm's ontology, Joanne and Henry are individuals bounded by their skin—bodies that have will, intentions, mental states, emotions etc. The body is also 'cut up' in separate compartments, such as emotion, cognition etc., where, for example, agency and consciousness reside. This makes it possible to refer to 'cognitive agency'. So, what might the story of Henry walking back from the shop be like in the World of Objects? A scientific realist interpretation of this clip might go something like this:

> We can see Henry, a 7-year-old child, triumphantly holding paper money in one hand and a roll of sticky tape in the other. His arms stretched out over his head express a clear sense of achievement. He must be delighted with his own initiative to go to the shop. His sense of autonomy and agency is enabled by initially observing and imitating adults and by their modelling of how to make a sack ball, how to go shopping and so forth.

In this interpretation of the clip, Henry is already configured as 'a child'—a young human. As he grows, Henry, who is still developing, will become more mature and eventually become a responsible citizen. This endpoint of the maturation process will only come with age. This young human is also an *individualised* being, ontologically a contained unit *in* space and time.

We do *see* the sticky tape and the paper money with our human eyes, but with our theoretical lenses only in the service of the humans who are going to the shops. The objects matter only when the material arrangement in its particularity helps us understand Henry's intentions and actions. Objects, such as sticky tape and money are passive, inert matter and need humans to give it agency. This theoretical lens also assumes that the world is a Newtonian spacetime container in which things happen. For physicist Isaac Newton, in terms of space, the world is one that comprises "individual objects with individually determinate properties, and measurements reveal the preexisting values of particular physical quantities" (Barad, 2007, p. 262). Child is a 'container' with limbs, attributes, properties, and an 'inner' and an 'outer'. Helena Pedersen poignantly observes that scientific classifications separate, identify, delimit, and fix things relative to other things, and as such structure a particular way of value-laden thinking about them, despite the sciences' claim to neutrality (Pedersen, 2010, Ch 1). In terms of time, Newton subscribed to the Democritean notion that nature only has two elements: atoms and the void. Twentieth-century physics challenges Newtonian meta/physics. We explore the difference and why it matters in the section on the World of Phenomena.

In the World of Objects, Henry is an object subjected to the laws of nature. In this paradigm, time "marches forward" (Barad, 2019b, p. 528) and external forces on the 'outside' influence how his body responds, and how he feels and thinks on the 'inside' (brain, mind). We interpret his actions against a backdrop of absolute space and universal time; neither time, nor space is 'situated' (as, e.g., argued by Haraway, 1988). The universal criteria we use to assess Henry's progress in digital play are objective and do not depend on the presence of the zinc, the smell of the protest smoke, the touch of the pyjamas Henry wears or the sound of the ocean nearby. These environmental factors would all matter for education scientists who work from the perspective of child-as-Subject to which we now turn. In a World of Subjects, the instruments that measure children's experiences as, for example, 'joyful' are also in a sense subjective, in that they are open for debate and disagreement among researchers, but the agencies of observation (the camera) does not change the data (see Chapter 6 for a detailed discussion about child agency).

The World of Subjects

We will now interpret the video clip (Figure 3.5) from the perspective of child-as-Subject—a radically different way of thinking about the human ontologically, that is, in its assumptions about what the human *is*. We strongly recommend watching the video clip again. Re-turning, we notice that the digital lens is focused on Henry in the centre of the clip. From this framework, Henry is the child who is valued and considered a citizen with rights and a voice (United Nations, 1989). However, the human lens that privileges autonomy, voice, and individual agency assumes a linear maturation process (white privilege). What is assumed in the children's rights discourse is that the end goal of childhood is the formation of an adult citizen competent and capable of living individually and contributing productively to a western-style liberal democracy (Murris & Reynolds, 2018). The child of the United Nations Convention on the Rights of the Child (UNCRC) is the western indoor child who is active, capable, visible, and powerful but in need of protection. This is unlike many children in Africa who have adult responsibilities, for example, in some child-led households in an informal settlement such as Vrygrond.

In the World of Subjects, an even more child-centred way of using the technology is to hold the GoPro at Henry's height or even let Henry wear the GoPro himself. Why indeed is Joanne holding it in her hands, rather than Henry? (See the discussion earlier about safety in Vrygrond.) Qualitative researchers claim that recordings made by GoPros worn by children, as in Eshal's case (Figure 3.2), offer data from the perspective of the child and thereby position child research participants as capable and as having a voice. We re-turn to the concept of 'voice' in the next chapter. At this point, it is worth mentioning the useful distinction between 'standpoint' and 'perspective'. Asbjørn Magnar Hov and Henrik Neegaard (2020) suggest that 'standpoint' is about "'adults' intentions and interpretations of what children need and think", whereby 'perspective' would lead us "to what the child actually sees and what actually appears as meaningful for the child" (Hov & Neegaard, 2020, p. 6). Through the visual medium, and because Eshal will be inclined to forget she is wearing a GoPro, while she is wearing one, her behaviour (body language, gestures, language etc.) will give Adult researchers access to her perspective. They would insist that despite being culturally constructed, the technology will provide 'naturalistic' data and unique insights while she is wearing it.

For constructionists and socio-constructivists, in the World of Subjects, *the eye of the camera is seen as extending the human eye* and assists the researcher in co-creating knowledge about other humans and the world. This perspective acknowledges *humans' inherent subjectivity* in creating and reading data that as such exists in the world but is ontologically *separate from the researcher.* The affordance of the technology to play the clip back repeatedly helps to make the analysis *intersubjective* and contestable. Knowledge is uncertain and open for negotiation and discussion by a team of qualitative researchers.

The child-as-Subject paradigm positions Henry and his identity as a product of his surroundings and social, geopolitical, economic, and cultural contexts. Paying attention to these helps us researchers understand his digital practices and those of his family better. Culture and context, including digital lenses, mediate our understanding of reality. Although the video clip was accidentally slowed down by Joanne's hand, we stopped the clip at a particular point. Henry is stretching both arms in the air holding the change for Joanne in one hand and the sticky tape in the other. Why did we use the lens in this way and for what purpose?

We were struck by Henry's gesture of triumph. Of course, this is a subjective interpretation, and from a child-as-Subject paradigm this is a *quality* of the research, not a hindrance or something negative. On the contrary, knowledge is always situated. Intersubjectively we can discuss each other's interpretation and dis/agree about it. An analogy would be to see the world as a house with many windows and each human researcher would be looking through their own window. We cannot look through other people's windows—like glasses that cannot be removed from our eyes. We can of course compare notes, but this knowledge of other people's experiences is by description and not by direct acquaintance—a useful distinction made by Bertrand Russell in 1910.[7] Such a comparison of how we describe what we observe and critically reflect on what we see and hear and use our lenses (whether our own eyes or the digital) is very typical of qualitative research. In a research method class, a lecturer might play the video clip as a starting point for an open-ended enquiry without insisting that there is one right interpretation of the event that happened in space and time.

Poststructuralists and socio-constructivists might argue that the lens in this clip is *colonial* in that readers are invited to look 'in' or 'down' on Henry by the angle of Joanne's GoPro lens. The child-as-Subject perspective is about distribution of power, egalitarianism, and negotiation of authority. The digital lens can be used for this purpose by humans. Let us re-turn to the clip and explore how we might narrate an interpretation from the child-of-Subject perspective:

'We'—Adult researchers and some of us with a white skin and none of us speaking Chichewa—notice a small-sized human of colour with a Black skin. We also record Henry's age and are struck by his independence and the strong relationships he has with other humans around him, his mother, Lily, and his dad, Henry Senior. Henry's agency is influenced by systems, how discourses work (surveillance, national curriculum, international regimes of testing etc.), environmental influences (sand, wind, ocean, small dwelling, health and safety risks etc.), and his identity (boy, Black, living in poverty, seven years old, fit and strong for his age, multilingual etc.). By slowing down and freezing these moments in space and time, the GoPro has made it possible to notice the many factors that influence his identity.

Using this holistic framework decolonises by affirming the importance of *identity* and the politics of childhood (see Table 3.1). In the sociology of childhood, such an affirmation of agency and strengthening Henry's voice by assigning rights to him (by adults) is paramount. For this human-centred lens, we can see how the child-as-Subject framework in the World of Subjects makes it possible to interpret both Henry and Eshal as agentic. However, it is dangerous to believe that we can undo our own authority and colonial gaze as researchers simply by changing the angle of a lens or by giving children GoPros to wear. Subjectivity in both ontological worlds, the World of Objects as well as the World of Subjects, assumes Newtonian notions of space and time (see above) and this is a very important difference with the next lens, marked by the so-called 'ontological turn' in postresearch (see Chapter 1).

The World of Phenomena

From the human optics lens of Newtonian physics, subjects and objects are discrete autonomous and bounded entities in the world *before* they are in relation with others. The Worlds of Object and Subject are human-centred worlds where knowledge production is built around language in the broad sense. Education focuses on how semiotic systems, such as language, visual images, concepts, audiotapes etc., *mediate* human access to the material world (Barad, 2007, p. 48). Adult intervention (mediating, guiding, instructing, diagnosing etc.) is brought into existence by the culture/nature binary (Murris, 2016).

The paradigms discussed so far assume the independent existence of objects and subjects that move through space (as a container) and forward in (unilinear) time. In terms of their theories of knowledge (epistemologies), these frameworks presuppose an independent and *external* world of bounded zipped subjects and objects known by a researcher *representationally* and cognitively through ideas and concepts *inside* the human mind. In contrast, in a World of Phenomena, subject and object are inseparable non-dualistic wholes (Barad, 2011, p. 143). The concept 'phenomenon' as used here, is not the same as the one used by phenomenologists. The latter puts the human body in the centre of deciding what is real. So, in that sense, their usage of phenomena belongs to the World of Subjects.

According to posthumanists, subject and object cannot be separated in reality; there are no insides or outsides to these bodies. In other words, the video clip is not a mere object of human knowledge. Nature does not exist 'out there', passively, to be discovered by humans' thinking about or experimenting on 'it'. For an agential realist, it is impossible to separate or isolate practices of knowing and being: "they are mutually implicated" as *a matter of fact* (Barad, 2007, p. 185). The location of the subject is also not stable, but in/determinate. To explore further the affordances of the small more-than-human such as the digital for seeing the child human differently in research, let us open up the video clip for further re-working.

From a quantum physicist's point of view, there is an "inherent ambiguity of bodily boundaries" (Barad, 2007, p. 155)—boundaries that only become determinate through specific practices. In that sense, identity is neither fixed nor inherent to an individual. So how would a posthumanist analysis work in the case of the video clip in Figure 3.5? (It is important to re-turn to the QR code and especially listen to the sounds this time.)

Henry is holding the banknote in one hand and the sticky tape roll in the other. For quantum physicist Niels Bohr, it depends on whether Henry is holding the objects loosely or not, because when held tightly he would have lost "the sensation that it is a foreign body" (Bohr in Barad, 2007, p. 154). An obvious objection might be that this is just a matter of how humans *experience* the world subjectively and not how things *are* in the world.[8] But Barad counters this possible objection; we in turn diffract the clip through their powerful argument (Barad, 2007, pp. 155–156). The outside boundary of Henry's body may seem evident, because it ends at the surface of his skin. But according to physical optics (not geometrical optics), boundaries are neither ontologically nor visually determinate. When we come to the 'edges' of a banknote, a GoPro or a hand, it is not that there are x number of atoms that belong to a hand, y number of atoms that belong to the banknote, and z number of atoms belong to the GoPro. Barad continues:

> Furthermore, as we have seen, there are actually no sharp edges visually either: it is a well-recognized fact of physical optics that if one looks closely at an "edge," what one sees is not a sharp boundary between light and dark but rather a series of light and dark bands—that is, a diffraction pattern.
>
> *(Barad, 2007, p. 156)*

So, for Barad, the production of bodily boundaries is not a matter of someone's individual, subjective experiences, or about how we *know* the world, but the way the world is put together *ontologically*. Barad is not just making the point that it is an empirical fact that there are 'clear boundaries' only for the human eye (therefore subjective) and that this is *not* the case from a physical optics point of view. They would most likely claim that the way Henry negotiates the banknote and sticky tape *as part of his body* is the "result of the repetition of (culturally and historically) specific bodily performances" (Barad, 2007, p. 155). The integral entanglement of the material and the discursive only gets *noticed* (which does not mean that in *reality* this is not *always* the case) when he gives the change to Joanne and puts the sticky tape roll on the cement floor. Importantly, we only struggle with seeing *the entanglement* between the human and more-than-human, because we already bring "an image of normal embodiment" to our interpretations (Barad, 2007, p. 158). Posthumanism invites researchers to pay attention to the paradigms they take for granted and question the ontological dimensions of their scientific practices (Barad, 2007, p. 42). Indeed, why does it matter for Henry and Eshal, Lily and Henry Senior for us researchers to adopt a posthumanist lens? What difference does it make to see the boundaries 'between' bodies as diffraction patterns and not as 'zipped' bodies?

Diffraction helps us create visual images that play with the eye—the eye of the camera and the human—and brings other details to the attention of the postqualitative researcher—details otherwise forgotten or ignored, but are all part of the phenomenon. The sound of the video clip in Figure 3.5 is slowed down even more through a soundscape in the QR code in Figure 3.6.

As a childlike, non-representational methodology, temporal diffraction breaks with the temporality of progress and developmentalism (Murris, 2022a, Ch 4). Here, the accidental slowing down of the video clip draws attention to what for human eyes are 'lifeless' objects: the sticky tape, paper money, the zinc walls, the cement, the sack ball, the sound, and so forth. In this posthumanist vignette, time and space as concepts and the work they do in research become more apparent. The more-than-human are part of the phenomenon that makes Henry's agency possible. The vignette illustrates how visual technology does not simply *accurately represent or conserve the past in the present*. Deleuze also argues that cinema has the potential to shape our ideas about how events unfold timewise and even time and progression itself

FIGURE 3.6 Soundscape with Henry

(Lazzaroto, 2007, p. 96). This is important for the analysis as it holds on to the idea that video is also about the past, but at the same time involves a transformative element through its ability to make new connections and thereby shape the future (Menning & Murris, 2023)—the event is not 'closed', but always open for iterative re-working.

Now why does this matter and for whom or what? Re-turning repeatedly to the video clip as part of this vignette helps to do justice to the intricate detail of *specific connectivity* (Barad, 2007) of reading Henry-as-phenomenon in all its complexity. The interpretation changes with each viewing and by staying with it, questions cascade. The analysis remains *temporally open* as an ongoing worlding process and leaves traces by be(com)ing affected by the experiences of bodies always already in relation. A research site (see Chapter 5) is so much more dynamic than 'scenery' or the mere backdrop for human agents, or a static space in which to 'collect' data. The accidental slowing down of the video helps to draw attention to the material conditions of production *and* creation of research data. It also helps us *ask prior questions*, for example, 'What is assumed to be true (*a priori*) before these scientific prac-tices, informed by these theories, get underway, for example, what we mean by 'human' or 'child' in *this* specific instance?'

The GoPro is an unfamiliar device for Joanne's hand so it takes control of the sticky taping and stories with time-lapse mode, which makes us aware of what might not be present to the human senses but is still sedimented in the flesh of the world. The harrowing sound (amplified in the QR code in Figure 3.6) works to draw attention to what else is going on and what we miss when we focus only on Henry as a 'zipped' body of a particular age or size (whether reading him 'in context' or not). One could even speculate that the sound frequencies do some interesting work here. The distortions sound like whales: a reminder of the ghostly presence of the whales that were hunted in False Bay. The whales are drowned out when we listen only to the sounds outside Henry's home and tune in to the sound of the ocean close to his home. But the whales are here (and not here); their call is with/in the time-lapse mode (for more, see Murris & Peers, 2022). Haunting lies precisely in its refusal to contain, define, or express the closure of what is present or silent. In this vignette the slowing down was accidental, but in posthumanist research this is also done on pur-pose, has a 'de-stabilising effect', and can disrupt majoritarian notions of child development and agency.

Importantly, it is the *phenomenon* that is agentic, not child-as-Subject nor child-as-Object. Posthumanism makes it possible to pay attention to the relata that are part of the phenomenon, in this case the tape, the sack ball, the zinc walls, the sound, the paper money, the GoPro, the ancestors *ad infinitum*. They are all mutually perform-ative transindividual agents. As multispecies theorist Pauliina Rautio (2013) points out: humans and other animals continually create the conditions for each other's existence and this includes the inanimate such as rocks and stones, grass, and the wind. We always find ourselves already intra-actively entangled with the more-than-human—with what we can see, with what is far away and what was, and what will be.

In disrupting the human 'eye', as well as the digital eye, it becomes possible to respond to multiple temporalities and places. For posthumanists, it is not only important to see what is present but also to notice what is absent or in/visible and to trouble the dominance of human vision in deciding what is real. Yet although identity is dispersed, diffracted, and materially threaded through the self in spacetime, it does not follow that identity is erased (Murris & Peers, 2022). It is critically important that Henry's skin is black, that he lives in poverty, and that his parents are migrants from Malawi.

Ironically, what our re-turning to 'the data' brings to the fore is the even more significantly important role the adult human plays in knowledge production. Agential realism exposes the ethico-political nature of the apparatuses that researchers use and the ontologies they assume.

Postqualitative research creates awareness of how the representational use of technology materialises power-producing binaries such as Language/world, Symbolic/reality, Culture/nature. De/colonising research involves becoming aware of the humanist nature of our perceptions and engrained binary ways of thinking. Video and audio technology also play a critical role in positioning children (MacLure et al., 2010) through the Adult/child binaries (Murris & Menning, 2019) that thrive on the nature-culture bifurcation (see Chapter 1). The challenge is to 'get to the mirror' and become aware of the (Adult) 'I' who represents nature through its interventions (Murris, 2016) and to engage fully with the material features of the discursive (MacLure, 2013). Technology allows us to postpone Adult human-centred interpretations that assume not only human exceptionalism (Menning et al., 2021), but importantly *Adult* human exceptionalism. At the same time, a postqualitative analysis is still *anthropo-situated* (see, Murris & Peers, 2022). Diffracting through Haraway's influential notion of 'situatedness', Barad shares the insight produced through the diffraction: "location cannot be about occupying a fixed position, …[and] may be usefully (con)figured as *specific connectivity*" (Barad, 2007, pp. 470–471 ftn 45). The human researcher is entangled with the video practices that are not considered as passive, observing, and measuring activities simply with an "improved human eye" (Menning & Murris, 2023). On the contrary, the *anthropos* is productive and performative in how a phenomenon materialises and how meaning is given to what is observed (Mengis et al., 2016, pp. 5–6). Technology is not an improvement of the human eye, but enables us to look diffractively at 'slices' of reality through endless replays, thereby doing more justice to the complexity of reality (Murris, 2022a). Knowledge is constructed through "direct material engagement with the world" and not by "standing at a distance and representing" the world (Barad, 2007, p. 49). In other words, this work is postdigital; when recording and documenting 'our' observations of digital play, we do not simply record objectively what is happening, thus dissolving the usual distinction between 'objective' and 'subjective'.

As authors, we are response-able for what we include and exclude in the stories we tell. We therefore deliberately create stories with textures (e.g., text, images, QR codes, editing, sound)—creating 'vignettes' of sorts. Stories are material entities with/in the world, for which we are accountable and it is important to tell different stories that allow the 'Other' to respond (Haraway, 1988). This is the work all of us need to do, but we are not alone in that endeavour. We are assisted by humans and other-than-human 'Others': cells, water, sand, sticky tape, GoPro, newspaper, burning tyres, ash, zinc, smoke, biscuits, pyjamas, barbed wire, washing, scissors, and so on.

Diffractively reading Henry's and Eshal's 'unzipped' bodies and dis/embodied materiality is part of the phenomenon we trace as researchers—a postqualitative move that keeps the child human of colour in play through thinking-with concepts such as 'child', 'erasure', and 'time lapse' (Barad, 2017c, p. 45). What our different analyses expose is not the erasure of the human when decentring the human in posthumanist research (see Murris & Osgood, 2022); on the contrary, it shows first of all how the apparatuses introduced by the Adult human researcher as 'research instruments' profoundly matter in terms of research 'findings'. With the movement of the GoPro we let ourselves be moved away from the anthropocentric inclination to gaze at children's black and brown bodies as containers of thought, intention and mental states—conceptualised as beings with (or without) agency. Instead, we turn to transmodal spatial and temporal diffractions of *visual* and *aural* texts that bounce like 'Henry's' sticky sackball and *perform* without a need for too elaborate (cognitive) *explanations* by the Adult human (Murris & Peers, 2022). When meeting the diffractive text, or rather, our compos(i)t(ion), its significance is what readers have "to find for themselves, by drawing them into correspondence with their own experience and life histories" (Ingold, 2018, p. 12).

In sum, unlike phenomenologists, posthuman researchers are not only disrupting what an object is, but also disrupting human-centred conceptualisations of the subject (anthropocentrism) and human exceptionalism, that is, locating knowledge, intelligence, and meaning-making *in* the individualised subject, and in the *human* subject only (Braidotti, 2013, 2018, 2022).

All knowledge-making practices, including the use of techno-logical apparatuses such as photography and video, are "material enactments that contribute to, and are a part of, the phenomenon we describe" (Barad, 2007, p. 32).

Cracking the lens

In this chapter, technology does the work of 'cracking' the repre-sentational lens described in Chapter 1 and above, and exposes the non-innocence of the lenses we use, and use us, as being more than a representation of reality-as-it-is. The lens itself in its materiality makes us think in a multiplicity of ways about the world as we have shown through a detailed analysis of two vignettes. Also inspired by Gilles Deleuze's philosophising about cinema, we technically choreographed selected data 'post' pro-duction, for example, by diffracting images through one another (Figures 3.2 and 3.3). Through and with the diffractive images we draw the attention of the viewer to objects, sounds, atmospheres and so on, and let ourselves be affected. Such experiences make it possible to disrupt normalised ways of knowing and seeing and reconfigure digital play.

The point is not to dissect an action in minute detail in an effort to better accurately describe and represent reality-as-it-is. On the contrary, by carefully selecting images (what Barad would call an 'agential cut'), technically manipulating them and reading some of them diffractively, we exposed the role technology plays in constructing a particular way of reading Henry's play—literally, but also metaphorically. In that sense, agential realism reconfigures the meaning of 'objectivity'. An educational researcher must *perform* in order to see; we learn to 'see' through the apparatuses that measure by *doing*, and not by seeing (Barad, 2007, p. 51). These performative practices are not only material, but also discursive and in reality are always entangled with our figurations of child and childhood (see e.g., Lenz Taguchi, 2010; Giorza, 2021).

Still and moving images are 'data' that are never 'set'. Like other bodies, video clips and photographs are not bounded, zipped 'things' but always already ontologically an "intra-active host of others" (Barad, 2017c, p. 36). As described in Chapter 1, this book *is* about a re-turning to the specks of our data sets that invoke the down-to-earth practices of the earthworm. What the diffractive images in this chapter offer is an 'extra eye'—an eye 'outside' human perception (Menning & Murris, 2023) opening the data up, letting the air in, and allowing it to become different. It is not the way our eyes work 'normally' speaking, but these visual manipulations work to decentre the child human and provoke profound questions about the use of technology in research and what it can tell us about the world and—in the context of this book—about children's digital play.

In the next chapter, we re-turn to how digital devices as research instruments to 'collect' data can cause other ethical problems. Continuing the focus on sound, but this time not sound created by the GoPro, we explore how human sounds are transcribed as part of the data. We re-turn to Henry's interview and show again how data 'collection' is never innocent, but material-discursive and the more-than-human are always threaded through. In education research, transcribers are usually not regarded as researchers, that is, involved in the theorising of a research project. In conversation with each other, we discuss the epistemological implications of the invisibility of transcribers and argue why it matters ethically and politically.

Notes

1 The children are two of the focus children from the CTAP project as described in Chapter 1.
2 See Chapter 1 and Figure 1.2
3 These are pseudonyms and the children's names have also been changed in the image.
4 This is a very rough estimate as the wages people earn who live in informal settlements and townships is difficult to trace and often falls outside the official statistics. See Business Tech (2021) article with estimates: https://businesstech.co.za/news/finance/493609/heres -how-much-money-people-in-cape-town-earn-based-on-where -they-live-and-work/
5 The concept 'inhuman' is not an erasure of difference between adult and child, or a flattening of boundaries between human and the more-than-human, or "extending the boundaries of the human," but signals "a transformation of humanism from within" (Truman, 2019, p. 5). Thinking-with the inhuman "points to the violence that the category of the human contains within itself" (Luciano and Chen quoted in Truman, 2019, p. 5). This idea of the inhuman is postdigital, and troubles the distinction we are making between human lenses and the lenses of machines as if they were completely separate (see Chapter 2).
6 For example, the use of Video Assistant Referee (VAR) during soccer matches assumes that the cameras from different angles record what actually happened on the field as a matter of fact. Although there can still be disagreements about whether what is recorded amounts to, e.g., 'a penalty', a 'red card' etc. as that requires human judgement against a set of criteria that govern fair play and the accurate applica-tion of the rules of the game. For example, it is not always easy to

discern whether the player dived (e.g., the video doesn't record the force of a push) or was really tackled in the penalty area.

7 See De Poe's (n.d) paper, 'Knowledge by Acquaintance and Knowledge by Description, in https://iep.utm.edu/knowacq/

8 Barad (2007, p. 159) illustrates this idea with an example of Stephen Hawking's motionless body when he gives a talk through an artificial speech device. Without the device (the box in his lap) there is no talk, no Hawking. Hawking does not stop at the edge of his body (Barad, 2007, p. 159). For Hawking talking about how 'he' talks: https://www.youtube.com/watch?v=UErbwiJH1dl

4

RECONFIGURING TRANSCRIPTION IN EDUCATIONAL RESEARCH

In conversation with transcribing

One of the aspects of data collection that became increasingly significant for us in the Children, Technology and Play (CTAP) project was that of transcription and researchers' intra-actions with transcribers. In this chapter, we reconfigure the concepts of transcriber and transcription through the postdigital and reconceptualise voice ('Voice without Organs'). We also disrupt conventional notions of language(s) and subjectivity. Following on from Chapter 3, we understand voice not as emanating from individuals but as a collective. Posthumanism decentres the human but without erasing geopolitically situated identities (Murris & Osgood, 2022). We playfully write this chapter as a non-linear transcribed conversation that unfolds between the five authors (and infinitely more unnamed ones), but our names don't signify specific bounded bodies located in space and time. At the same time, the *placing* of 'our' names in the dialogue isn't random either. How languages and languaging work profoundly affect the power relations we

DOI: 10.4324/9781003205036-4

attune to in agential realism; race, gender, and age all matter. We diffract through transcripts from the CTAP data and "walk around in our conceptual distinctions" (Barad in Barad & Gandorfer, 2021, p. 31). 'Language' itself as a concept is reconfigured as more-than-language: language *is* home, it is a *being and becoming with-in* the language. Opening some key concepts up and burrowing through tunnels, this re-storying mobilises decolonising moves in education research.

We re-turn to Chanique's joining the CTAP project half-way as a transcriber and translator of some of the fieldwork data.

Chanique: Joining the project when most of the fieldwork was already completed was daunting, the researchers already had an established relationship with the case study families. I remember an intense feeling of urgency and the weight of a looming project deadline. Being completely in the dark about what exactly was needed from me was a little scary, but I was happy to journey with Joanne and the beautiful stories of Eshal, her mother, and her sister.

Joanne: You definitely joined the project at a chaotic time! The data files were growing at a rate that transcribers could not keep up with and selecting data for transcribing was challenging because it coincided with field visits for researchers. On top of that, some fieldworkers had limited transcription experience. This meant that their transcripts would need reviewing and editing. The pressure was on us to have the transcripts finished so that the analysis could be completed and the report written. We needed to bring other transcribers on board to keep us moving towards the fast-approaching deadline.

Chanique: [laughs] This was the first time I had worked on an education research project but at least I had been working as a transcriber for five years and had my fair share of transcription experiences! Even so, it is challenging coming into a project mid-flow and trying to get a sense of it. Too often, in my experience, transcribers are a part of creating stories about research that we do not really know much about—because we are not considered to be part of the research team!

Kerryn: Following on from that comment Chanique, one of the things we have talked about a lot as a group is how we have been affected by the transcripts, but particularly the interviews, videos, voicenotes, and GoPro recordings that you transcribed. The creation (and important re-creation) of transcripts, which we will talk about in a bit, as well as their ongoing presence is something we keep re-turning to. They are more than individual voices of participants typed out on pages. Your previous experiences as a transcriber have really been helpful in troubling not just transcription and the role of transcribers in research but also our ongoing troubling of data.

Chanique: Transcribing for me, has always been quite a sticky process. Honestly, I struggled with it when I first started transcribing. I did not like the one-dimensional view of transcription where it is seen as simply the "process of converting speech from an audio or video recording into text" (Hall, 1997, p, 37). As if that is a simple mechanical task! This view is also based on the idea that transcription is a linear process that works within predefined and standardised linguistic parameters. Of course, I am not saying that this is the only way transcription is done, because it is not, or that there is not a fair amount of debate in the field. But when I began transcribing it felt a bit odd, like something outside of me. And, I think that stems from the fact that I am an Afrikaaps speaker (see page 131). Transcription was a sticky process because I had to adapt *my* mother tongue to be able to be a 'professional' transcriber – whatever that actually means! I had to learn to exclude utterances, repetitions, and worldly sounds. Anything that did not 'fit' into those standardised linguistic parameters – you know – what's considered 'proper language'. That's the problem with seeing transcription as a representational practice that privileges language – it doesn't take account of the 'other', whether it is the sound of a pin dropping, or repetition, or translanguaging,[1] or the unsaid that is communicated through things like nonverbal movements, physical orientations, marginalised languages, and the more-than-human.

Kerryn: Your experience highlights an assumption that the people who are creating these transcripts are objective data capturers who are placed outside of the messiness and dilemmas that are always a part of the research process. And as you say, so often transcribers working on qualitative research projects tend to be excluded in terms of co-creating, shaping, and reshaping data. But transcribers *are* part of making the data that are analysed and written into research papers. For us, the role of the transcriber and the creation of new material artefacts and the positioning of 'othered' voices are central to the material-discursive apparatus (Barad, 2007) in educational research.

Karin: Yes. As we have been talking about in the book, an 'apparatus' for Barad (2007, p. 183) is "a doing, not a thing"—a performative practice. When understood as apparatuses, it becomes clearer that video and audio recordings and how they are transcribed are boundary-making practices. The analysis of the vignettes in Chapter 3 shows how digital lenses are not simply objects or passive 'matter'. Matter is not simply an 'inanimate given' or 'mere stuff' that is unresponsive and in need of something else 'to give' it agency or 'an inert static canvas' without "memory, history, or an inheritance to call its own," waiting to be inscribed by human meaning and culture (Barad, 2013, p. 17). Human metaphorical (and digital) lenses shape what is noticed and counts as important data and therefore needs to be transcribed according to the researchers. Transcribers are also entangled in the research paradigms researchers inhabit.

Chanique: I think I have been working mainly with researchers who inhabit what we have been calling the 'World of Objects', or the scientific realism paradigm. Transcripts in *that* world are things that capture events in the world so that they can be ready for analysis by researchers. Transcription is a mechanistic process. Data exist separately from the researcher 'out there in the world'. It's the same for researchers who inhabit the 'World of Subjects' or the constructionist and socio-constructivist paradigm. However the relationship to knowledge in the 'World of Subjects' is different. Knowledge is co-constructed.

Researchers in this World use my transcripts to create knowledge about the world but acknowledge that there *is* a level of subjectivity in how they interpret the transcripts. Depending on the researcher, they may also acknowledge that my position as transcriber isn't neutral. I like how Mary Bucholtz (2000, p. 1440) talks about this. Wait, let me read this to you:

All transcripts take sides, enabling certain interpretations, advancing particular interests, favoring specific speakers, and so on. The choices made in transcription link the transcript to the context in which it is intended to be read. Embedded in the details of transcription are indications of purpose, audience, and the position of the transcriber toward the text. Transcripts thus testify to the circumstances of their creation and intended use. As long as we seek a transcription practice that is independent of its own history rather than looking closely at how transcripts operate politically, we will perpetuate the erroneous belief that an objective transcription is possible.

Theresa: So, the questions we are asking here are:
- What do transcripts 'do' in the 'World of Phenomena'?
- How do they work differently within a posthumanist and agential realist paradigm?
- How does thinking-with transcripts and posthumanism reconfigure the concepts of transcription and transcriber?

Karin: These are very helpful questions, Theresa. As we've been arguing in the book in relation to data, transcripts are not separate from the researcher or the transcriber. They are part of the world, material-discursive apparatuses. They 'do' work in the world, that's Barad's (2007) point about performative practices. They are not inert or lifeless as Koro-Ljungberg (2018) and her colleagues remind us—and they certainly have not been in this project!

Joanne: In their creation and recreation, they live in our ears and eyes and watery bodies. Transcripts are co-constituters of the world (van Dooren & Rose, 2016).

Kerryn: In other words then, interviews and transcription are a ubiquitous part of qualitative research. Let's stay with what is often seen as an unproblematic practice (Point & Baruch, 2023), something that gets done before the real analytical work begins.

Disturbing (human) voice(s)

Joanne: Chanique, you started with Eshal's files. It was mid-fieldwork when home visits were well on their way. The transcriber who was working with our research group didn't have enough hours to cover the transcribing that was needed. I think I sent you voice note files from Eshal's WhatsApp group. It might have been my way to lure you in!

Chanique: Yes! Those voice notes were like octopus tentacles pulling me in. The familiarity of your voice in those WhatsApp voice notes helped to win me over, so to speak (see Chapter 5). To hear the sound of Eshal, Rihana, and your voice, akin to mine … Also, Eshal was unassumingly brilliant in how she questioned everything that you sent her way. And that was the challenge, to capture her liveliness, to make the transcript tell the story that traditional transcription couldn't fully capture. It immediately became so much more than just work.

Joanne: I appreciate what you're saying. Can you keep going with that thought?

Chanique: Well, like I said before, my experience has been transcribing files without connections beyond the sound of the audio in the files. I was suddenly aware of the concept of affect. I could not escape from relations beyond the sound. For example, accents, mother and child intra-actions between Rihana and Eshal, and the sense of community between this family and the researchers. I can't quite explain it but there was way more going on for me than typing words that I was hearing in an audio file.

Kerryn: Listening to you makes me think about how bizarre it is that transcribers are considered passive in the world of research. Like you are just part of the machinery of transcription. As researchers on a team, we have conversations about the interviews, or parts of interviews that move or shock or disturb us, or throw up something really exciting. But if you are seen as outsourced labour you are excluded from these important conversations. Of course, I suppose, some people may argue that as a 'professional' it is not your job to be 'affected' in the World of Objects. Or they may acknowledge that you may find the stories interesting but you need to separate the cognitive from the rest of your self (that mind-body split). And that highlights the issue of language—you get paid to put down words and the researchers deal with the rest.

Karin: This brings me back to what we argued for in Chapter 3. And we are back again in the Worlds of Objects and Subjects where language holds a dominant and privileged position. In these human-centred worlds, language is central to how knowledge is produced. Barad (2007) reminds us that it is problematic to think that there is an independent reality 'out there' separate from our descriptions of it, or the Constructivist view that reality is discursively mediated. The world is not represented through language only but comes to matter through dynamic intra-actions between humans, language, and materiality.

Kerryn: Yes, that means that we need to think about language differently. When you describe what happens when you listen to the recordings of Rihana and Eshal, it is so much more than a narrow view of language and the related practices of transcription you were trained to use. I really like Pennycook's (2018, p. 455) reminder that we need to move beyond "standard linguistic assumptions—that the linguistic sign is arbitrary, that words have meanings, that grammar has rules, *that languages exist*, that we need to speak the *same language* to communicate." Instead we should be thinking about communication in broader more open-ended ways. But, as Karin keeps pointing out in her scholarship, we are constantly learning from children about the ways in which they use 'a hundred languages and a thousand more' when making meaning (Murris, 2016). Language is not central to communication because it is only one part of a whole range of semiotic (Pennycook, 2018) and material-discursive (Barad, 2007) possibilities. Like pregnancy!

Chanique: Exactly! I was in my third trimester and heavily pregnant when I started the transcriptions. There was this intensity in the listening as I was pulled in by Eshal and Rihana's voices. My whole body was moved by these conversations. Eliana-in-utero and I were listening to these mother-daughter moments together. I know the official focus of the project was on children's play and the project emphasised children's perspectives but there were *so* many moments where mothering was amplified. The warmth, love, and care that enveloped Rihana's daughters settled into the foreground. I (with Eliana) was drawn to Rihana's voice, and her gentle coaching of Eshal as she supported her in her answers. Rihana's whispers seemed so quiet but so vital. I realised when I was finishing some of the transcripts that her voice and relations with Eshal were left out because the focus was on what Eshal was saying. I reinserted what Rihana said. Like in this extract:

Eshal: *Good evening Mrs Peers. It's me Eshal. How are you today? So today, I went to the library and took the GoPro with and they took a video of me in the library. Uh-uh, a video of me in the library and they also took of the liba- libra-rian. Li-bra- It's hard to pronounce it. Li-bra-rian, li-bra…*

Rihana: *-rians, librarian.*

Eshal: *Uh librarians and I, my- I went there to go get books.*
              So, I took a video of it.

Rihana: *I made a video…*

For me, Eshal and Rihana were one body, which resonated with my pregnancy and disturbed these omissions. These 'background' murmurs were not insignificant; it was the timbre of generations of women's love. It was sensory, a connection with Eliana's movements which couldn't be heard, but seen and felt.

Joanne: I'm really moved by what you're saying Chanique. [General murmurs of agreement…]

Theresa: We've used the word 'voice' several times already and sometimes quite colloquially where it is an individual utterance produced by our bodies to make meaning, or voice is actually a synonym for language. Can we pause for a moment to talk about voice from a posthumanist perspective—the World of Phenomena, if you like? Voice in this World doesn't refer only to words that come out of a human's mouth. It's also not connected to the way some qualitative researchers in the World of Subjects use it when they say things like, 'the voice of the child' or that they want to let the voices of silenced groups like children 'be heard'. This is often connected to participatory methodologies, where the 'voices' elicited are children's perspectives of the world that researchers interpret (e.g., see Clark et al., 2014; Percy-Smith & Thomas, 2009).

Karin: Thanks Theresa, what comes to mind is Lisa Mazzei's (2013, p. 733) concept of the "Voice without Organs" inspired by Deleuze's idea of "thinking without organs." Mazzei and Alecia Youngblood Jackson problematise research that assumes that using the exact words of participants (even if it includes paralinguistic cues like pauses or stutters), gets at the 'truth' of our experiences. They argue that this thinking assumes that voices are "stable, present, authentic and self-reflective. Voice is still 'there' to search for, retrieve and liberate" (Mazzei & Jackson, 2012, p. 746). It also privileges the Humanist subject as the only being who has a voice because they have language.

Kerryn: Yes … exactly. What we are saying then is that voice pre-exists individual expression—which means that it is decoupled from a Humanist subject. That goes back to the argument we made in Chapter 1, and we return to in Chapter 6; voice, and therefore agency and intentionality, are always produced in relation with material-discursive human and more-than-human others. For Mazzei (2016, p. 154) voice is "a process of couplings and connections of different bodies, places, spaces, times, utterances, and becomings."

More-than-human voices

Joanne: Through this conversation, voice becomes something different and I am suddenly thinking about Henry making the sackball during one of the home visits (see Chapter 3). What are the "couplings and connections of bodies, time, spaces, utterances and becomings" (Mazzei, 2016, p. 154) when we re-turn to the sackball (Figure 4.1)?

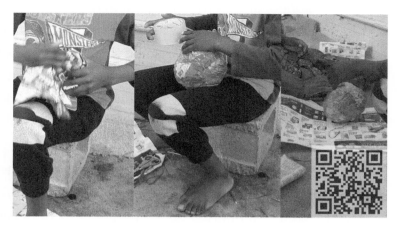

FIGURE 4.1   Re-playing the sackball

Chanique: The first time I watched the video for Henry's home visit,
the laughter and sounds of my childhood vividly became
part of the present. Growing up, children would gather on
the road for a game of *Skalulu*,[2] hoping that at least one of
the children would have a ball to play with. Many times
nobody had a ball so everyone was instructed to bring as
many *sakkies* (plastic bags), those who did not have bags
brought sticky tape or stockings. All of these household
items would then become the sackball. And, it was *majestic*, it created a space to play, but more than that it became
its own phenomenon, something that connected generations and many diverse communities around South Africa.
The sheer will and determination to play illustrates children's resourcefulness and capabilities.

Theresa: Yoh, I love how the sheer materiality of the ball, the
newspaper, the sticky tape on the video recording
affected you in this way. I wonder if another transcriber
had watched that recording how the sackball may have

been storied, and to what extent it may have only been seen as something that grew from a resource-constrained environment. Yet, what you are saying Chanique is that it is so much more. In fact, this sackball is clearly entangled with intra-generational histories of childhoods in Africa and in that sense agentic and part of 'your' voice.

Chanique: Oh, do you mean the sackball has a voice?

Theresa: No, what I am saying is that the vignette really helps rethink space and time when we talk about voice. So, you weren't transported back in time as such, because that would imply that remembering is unilinear, but the sackball is part of the story of the (world)making. In that sense it 'has' a voice and is agentic as part of the complex phenomenon that is socio-material, and er…

Joanne: Historical.

Kerryn: And cultural.

Karin: Uh, economic too.

Chanique: Also political.

Theresa: And geographic and scientific …

Chanique: Sure, but *language* also really *matters*. I found myself going back to the transcripts and the video data because some of the transcripts I worked with had not been completed by a transcriber or one of the research team had asked for additional transcripts. What really stood out for me was the disparity between transcripts and audio/video files. It is as if something was amiss. When I picked up omissions or language corrections I could not move forward by simply completing transcripts. It was not just Eshal's transcripts; the transcripts from Henry's video and audio files had similar silences and erasures.

Joanne: Your drawing our attention to these silences and erasures was a turning point for us! The sackball bounced us right into 'thick' conversations and made us pay attention to the politics of erasure and the ways in which we are implicated as researchers (see also Murris & Peers, 2022).

Chanique: Here is one of those moments ... It was during the home visit when Henry was making the sackball and ran out of sticky tape. He turns to his mother [Lily] and they have a conversation between themselves. Listen to this (Figure 4.2):

In the original transcript it says Lily and Henry are having a conversation in their home language:

Lily: Tape's finish.

Joanne: The only tape I had.

Lily and Henry have a conversation in their home language.

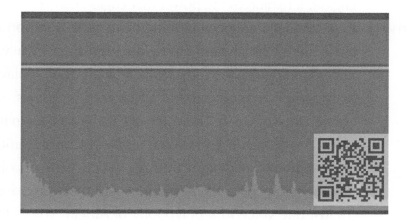

FIGURE 4.2 Audio recording of making the sackball

Lily:	I'm going to buy other tape.
Joanne:	Have you got other tape?
Lily:	I want to buy there.
Lily:	Where?
Lily:	There, the Somalia shop.

What language are they speaking? Does it have a name? Or is it merely *not English* and therefore not mentioned?

Karin: Sorry, what do you mean by 'not English', Chanique?

Chanique: A power-producing binary operates here where a non-dominant language is named in relation to a dominant language. English sits before the forward slash and all other African languages that are not English after the forward slash (English/not-English). This monoglossic orientation erases the translingual reality of this family in its specificity and community. The sentence in the original transcript, "Lily and Henry have a conversation in their home language," assumes that the language they speak does not matter, it has no name, it is invisible and exists outside of English. It reinforces the power that English carries.

Kerryn: If we are talking specificity then I think it is important to say here that Lily and Henry are speaking Chichewa. Did you know it's the most spoken language in Malawi? Its presence is another part of Mazzei's couplings and connections of voice. The voice of Chichewa lives in this place, Vrygrond. It carries the stories of displacement and economic migration through Africa with ongoing reverberations of colonial histories and their languages. It's just one voice in a polyphony of African voices that reverberate in this informal settlement. You are just as likely to hear a number of other African languages moving and flowing in translanguaging intra-actions with the 11 'official' South African languages and their local varieties. Chichewa is more than just a 'home language', a term that Makalela (2018) reminds us operates as a way of siloing languages.

Chanique: And Henry and Lily have to live every day within the borders of English. This moment flashes up (Barad, 2017c) how much power English carries, also within research and illuminates the need to re-think how research is designed from the outset, especially within multilingual communities. Although this is the case across the world, in South Africa the fact that 'minority' languages exist only in comparison with the colonial language of English is particularly poignant. It goes back to the binary I just spoke about.

Theresa: Yes, and we are realising more and more how transcribing and translating are intricately entangled with what counts as research data. And we know that transcribers hear things differently and make decisions about what to include and exclude so transcribing is an act of creating. But it is more complex than that. The way we had been working places the transcriber *outside* the team that does the research.

Karin: Even in the financial administration of the project, the transcribers and translators are 'service providers', not researchers.

Joanne: And this has profound implications for how we do research with children, especially in the global south.

Karin: I am thinking about how we do budgets at universities for projects such as CTAP and the politics of it. And, talking about implications for science, it affects how knowledge is produced. When adding items to the budget as Principal Investigator, it is unfortunately 'normal' to include transcribers and translators *after* the fieldwork has happened! The unilinearity of a project is simply assumed. This is also the case with the geopolitical points you've all been making. The research design couldn't have taken account of the multilingualism of Henry's family and the complexity of living and working in an informal settlement such as Vrygrond, as we discuss in Chapters 3 and 5.

Kerryn: If the starting point for research is that multilingualism is the global norm, we then can see the ways in which monoglossic orientations to the world are inscribed in institutional practices and have their own colonising force. And we can re-think research practices.

Karin: Agreed, these designs are supposedly universal and can be applied to all settings, simply by doing some 'tweaking'. And yes, of course, cultural, racial, ethnic, and linguistic differences can be taken into account in socio-cultural studies such as CTAP. But, through our iterative re-turning to the data, a very different storying unfolds.

Kerryn: Re-turning to Henry's home visit opens up the possibilities for flashing up (Barad, 2017a) the entangled historicity of the sackball. The inclusion of other soundscapes works to re-imagine the history and power that language carries. None of this would however be possible without the digital.

Theresa: Ah, postdigital worldings! We can chat about that too.

Joanne: Slow down Theresa! There is another phenomenon we need to have a conversation with before we go to the postdigital.

Theresa: Well, the postdigital has actually been here the whole time! But go ahead…

Decolonial voices: the bompie

Joanne: Chanique! Do you remember finding bompie? It was such an incredible moment for us! Afrikaaps suddenly manoeuvred its way in. Which is actually a strange thing to say because it was actually always already 'there', but also 'not there' at the same time in the transcript. It was pushed to the 'background' and made invisible. Then there it was again, pulsing in the video recording.

Chanique: There is so much we need to talk about! Is this the part you mean:

> *Henry:* Bompie.
>
> *Joanne:* Bompies, for who? A Bompie for who?
>
> *Henry:* For me.
>
> *Joanne:* For you and what about for Ma Lily? No Bompies for Lily? Explain, do you want to explain to Heloisa and Luzia. They don't know what a Bompie is. What is a Bompie, explain a Bompie to them.
>
> *Henry:* Something, something…
>
> *Luzia:* What?
>
> *Joanne:* Okay, describe what it looks like. Okay, and what's inside?
>
> *Henry:* Water.
>
> *Joanne:* And, where does that water live?
>
> *Henry:* They put apple inside.

> Joanne: They put an apple flavouring inside and then what do they do with the water once it's in there with an apple flavour?
>
> Henry: They put it on the freezer.
>
> Joanne: They put it in the freezer.
>
> Luzia and Heloisa: Ahhhhh.
>
> Joanne: What do you call it in Brazil?
>
> Luzia: Gelhino.

Joanne: Yes! In the World of Phenomena, language is not representational where the word bompie does not only refer to a frozen confectionery or ice lolly in the world. Instead, thinking-with bompie enables us to respond to the multiple temporalities and places it is entangled with, as well as the absences in the transcripts. In Chapter 1, we talked about how human-centred discourses put a particular Human (white, male, adult, able-bodied, heterosexual etc.) in the 'foreground' and put 'the rest' into 'the background': the normative language He (the ideal Human) is speaking. I want to argue that this is what happened with the bompie transcript. A white, colonial discourse that manifests in standardised, and I would say racialised, forms of language. It erases not just Chichewa but Afrikaaps. Afrikaaps is not to be confused with Afrikaans, one of South Africa's official languages.

Chanique: When I think of Afrikaaps, I don't think of it being a language. I think of growing up playing in the street, I think of the aunties sitting on the 'stoep' with a koesister.[3] I think of home. Afrikaaps is me. It is all the upheaval and the ultimate survival against adversity and oppression.

There is no Afrikaaps without colonisation. And I think that creates a special bond with its communities. I mean, yes, you have the linguistic aspect of Afrikaaps being a mixture of Indigenous San languages which comes from the Indigenous peoples whose relationship with Africa is thousands of years old. Then there is also the entanglement with Malay that comes from the enslaved people who were brought to the Cape as part of the colonisation by the Dutch. And of course, there is the Dutch. Afrikaaps is through and through a disruption of the binaries of standardised and informal varieties. The language in itself is just as colourful and vast as the houses in the Bo-Kaap.[4]

Joanne: I connect with the way you speak Chanique. It is an ontological thing. It is not just about knowing *how* to speak the language, but it is a *being and becoming within* the language. Already in Chapter 1, we talk about this and it is so important we come back to it in Chapter 5: 'we' are haunted by 'the' past and by futures. As Astrid Schrader (2012) points out, it is necessary to introduce haunting into the very construction of each concept, including 'being' and 'time'. It definitely resonates with the unboundedness and multiplicities of Afrikaaps.

Too often the limiting question people ask is: What is Afrikaaps? This question sets Afrikaaps up for simplification and finite expressions as you said. I really like what Adam Small says:

Kaaps is a language in the sense that it carries the whole fate and destiny of the people who speak it: the whole fate, their whole life 'with everything therein'; a language in the sense that the people who speak it, give their first cry in this life in this language, all the transactions of their lives are concluded in this language, their death rattle is rattled in this language. Kaaps is not a joke or a comedy, but a language.

(Small, 1973, p. 9, in Willemse, 2016, p. 75)

Theresa: There is a valuable documentary called *Afrikaaps* (Valley, 2010) which was produced a few years ago. The multimodal documentary brings together hip-hop, art practices, and stage performance. The director Dylan Valley works with the members of the project to politically complexify assumptions about Afrikaaps. Here's the link to the film: https://www.youtube.com/watch?v =WxMponKKsdc/.

Kerryn: I think it is a really powerful counter-narrative that challenges the position of white standard Afrikaans that only came to be through the work of the Apartheid state. The documentary, along with Afrikaaps, decolonises dominant narratives about what languages are, who speaks them, and what is 'correct' or 'proper' use of a language. It shows up dominant narratives of languages as stable and fixed, separate from the world, as a fiction. Afrikaaps is a *doing with* languages over centuries that is present in each utterance. It is also a language of resistance, silences, and marginalisation, as chronological periods melt, like the bompie, re-shaping and living inside communities. Some might argue that this is merely the subjective experiences of Afrikaaps speakers like Chanique and Joanne. It is that, *and* more than that! It is "the way the world is experiencing itself too" (Barad,2019b).

Joanne: Can I just say that the "world experiencing itself" (Barad, 2019b) is also about joy in everyday matterings. And those matterings are not just about children enjoying a bompie on a hot day. It's about our excitement at finding Heavy-Gpark's (2023) music video *Bompies* online. Which makes this the only chapter with its own official soundtrack and soundwave! (https://www.youtube.com/watch?v=rfOYMuSbh-U). And of course, there's the proliferation of TikTok videos on how to make homemade bompies.

Karin: Well listening to all of you speak, bompie is clearly an entanglement of more than just apple juice and water! It is such a boundary-breaking conversation that also engages with the complexity of what it means to *decentre* the human in posthumanist research *without erasing* the human, particularly because child is still so forgotten. In Chapter 3 of course, we show how focusing on the lenses we (adults) use and how digital lenses use us (humans) in research make us think differently about analysing data. There is an important connection here with how bompie is also co-constituted with the postdigital.

Postdigital voices

Kerryn: So, Theresa, you mentioned the postdigital being present in this conversation. How does a postdigital perspective help us reconfigure transcribing?

Theresa: I want to repeat the point we made in Chapter 2. The world is unavoidably digital but it is not the device or technology that marks the digital. There is a flexible shifting of relations or "interfacing" (Apperley et al., 2017) with the material, immaterial, human, and non-human, constantly falling in and out of intra-action. This fluidity brings to the practice of transcription an openness to listening differently, perhaps, in the way that Chanique as transcriber refuses the role of invisible 'service provider' and enters meaningful mutual intra-action with the data, voices, researchers, stories, places, and histories.

Kerryn: And transcribing work moves between the binaries, the digital, analogue, technological, non-technological, biological, and informational (Jandrić et al., 2018) it all intermixes. If we just think about transcription in this project, smartphones and GoPros recorded both audio and video of human and more-than-human participants—some human fingers help the recording with less dexterity than others like Slowing down Henry (Figure 3.5)! The recordings were downloaded and uploaded onto memory sticks, hard drives, laptops, and onto the Open Science Framework (OSF) project management tool so that the whole team could access files. Files multiplied as transcribers turned audio and video into words, becoming something new as they were re-created in another semiotic mode. Email threads emerged, sometimes going in circles hunting down missing files. As some of us printed transcripts, decorating them with pens and post-its, some of us read them online. They were read with, through and against other transcriptions, photographs, videos, drawings, collages, and other artefacts made in the focus groups. They've called out responses, sometimes of surprise, wonder, and curiosity. Some of them sent us back to listen to and watch the recordings again. Discussions about transcripts continued off the pages of the report, and these chapters and became lively discussions on Zoom, and WhatsApp.

Joanne: We cannot only focus on 'what' transcribers do without considering how they are part of broader research practices which include funding. That line item for transcription sitting on an Excel spreadsheet enables or constrains us.

Theresa: There is a push for researchers, and postgraduate students for that matter, to make use of transcription software that uses Automatic Speech Recognition (ASR) to save time and money.

Karin: Online Transcription software programmes can be downloaded for free or can be purchased at a fraction of the price human transcribers charge. It is very tempting to use them for transcribing recordings if you are pushed for time and have budget constraints. For example, someone pointed out a programme called *Descript* to me and it looks very promising I have to say. I know transcribers who use these programmes and just edit the English after using the software first.

Chanique: But Karin, what the examples of the sackball and the bompie show, is that machine transcription should not make human transcribers obsolete. It is critical to have transcribers who are situated within the communities they are researching.

Karin: True Chanique. This is what some of the CTAP transcribers thought as well. When we received the initial transcripts of some of the home visits and teacher interviews it became soon clear these tapes had not been transcribed by a human. Although technically speaking, a transcript, in the sense that words followed one another on a page, they were completely incomprehensible!

Chanique: While machine transcription obviously has affordances and can make us more efficient, I think, like play, it has a dark side that we need to burrow into a bit more. It is not a neutral tool. We know it silences the more-than-human voices and ends up giving a flat re-telling of an event. As a material-discursive doing it is bound up in monoglossic orientations to language that see languages as bounded. Why were those transcripts incomprehensible? Because programmes themselves are affected by these discursive constructions. The programmes have material affects: they are coded with ideal speakers in mind who speak standard forms of dominant languages with a particular accent and pronunciation. They mis-hear speakers who have other accents and speak other varieties. When you add other languages into the mix the transcripts are incomprehensible. This is a world where languages are separate entities, not a multilingual one where translanguaging happens all the time. It cannot hear the world of Afrikaaps. For me, that is the reproduction of colonial forms of power that are written into the code. We need to acknowledge the ways we are implicated in this kind of worlding. Am I saying don't use it?, No, because I do. But I want to do it response-ably.

Theresa: I think the postdigital is about dwelling in a place where the binaries of redemption (through the digital) on the one hand and 'dehumanisation' and similar negative fates on the other are no longer relevant.

Joanne: Yes, the digital is part of our reality and our survival and our getting on well (living and dying well in the words of Donna Haraway) will not depend on this or that technology but on our relations of care and kin-making. So maybe we just need to slow down and stay with the trouble!

Multiplying voices in research

Kerryn: How has staying with the concept of a transcriber and transcripts as part of slow scholarship enabled us to not just reconfigure these concepts but to do research differently?

Karin: Tracing the phenomena of the sackball and the bompie in their specificity flashes up some important insights into the decolonial reorientation of doing education research in the global south. Interestingly, our conversations aren't only about race and age, when meeting Henry and Eshal in Chapter 3, but also about gender when we meet Della in Chapters 2 and 6. Gender is of course also threaded through the storying of Eshal, Rihana, Chanique, Joanne, and unborn Eliana. But what this chapter throws up is how colonising language practices: race, gender, age, and language are all entangled when tracing how voice works in transcribing! Maybe expressed through individual mouths, but collectively produced.

Theresa: For sure, the tracing has helped us attune to multilingual transcribers moving beyond the sound of human voices. What you are saying Karin reminds me of an article by Lou Harvey, Paul Cook, and The Bishop Simeon Trust's (2021) about their research on Safe Spaces in Peace Education across Ekurhuleni Municipality on the outskirts of Johannesburg and how they work with children 'beyond' language. In their theorising, they draw on Bakhtin and here is a really helpful quote: "voice is material and immanent in the lived moment of the utterance (which may be linguistic but may also be a gesture, a look, an object, a silence)" (2021, p. 5). It gives 'home language' an entirely different meaning, doesn't it?

Kerryn: Yes! 'Home language' is part of more-than-human relations and involves an ontological turn. What Chanique was saying about Afrikaaps made us all think, didn't it, about how 'language' itself as a concept is reconfigured as more-than-language: language *is* home, it is a *being and becoming with-in* the language. This chapter, this re-storying, mobilises decolonising moves in education research. Afrikaaps for her is 'being home'. It involves a 'Voice without Organs', that is, going beyond the primacy of the word, connecting with her embedded and embodied situatedness in Cloetesville. We write about it in Chapter 7, quoting you Theresa! How moving away from the Humanist subject can lead to more poetic research calling up "other earthly creatures" (Giorza, 2021, p. 32).

Joanne: Of course, situatedness doesn't just mean 'location'. The embeddedness is fluid, like one's place in the Internet, or like seaweed in the ocean. It is time to swim into the watery worldings in the next chapter!

Notes

1 Translanguaging refers to the use of language systems by speakers in multilingual contexts that are strategic and situation sensitive. The emphasis is on 'languaging' that places the focus on what speakers *do* with languages. rather than the languages themselves' (Garcia, 2011, p. 17). Translanguaging challenges monoglossic ideas that languages are fixed, separate and static entities that are embedded in Enlightenment and colonial thinking (Makalela, 2018) and thus has decolonising potential. Makalela argues that the "fluid, porous, and flexible" use of language systems is relational; a force that creates new discursive systems as it disrupts monoglossic hierarchies (Makalela, 2018, p. 4).

2 Skalulu is a game I (Chanique) played growing up in Cloetesville, Stellenbosch in the Western Cape. We would gather all the kids in the road, it could be 5 or 25. We would then split into two equal teams. One team gets to run and one gets to kick. There are two goal lines and you run between them to gain points. You can run as long as no one from the opposing team catches the ball and hits you with it. This continues until the last person has been caught out. Then the sides switch.

3 A Cape Malay fermented spiced sweet dough that is fried in oil and then rolled in syrup and coconut.

4 https://www.sahistory.org.za/place/bo-kaap-cape-town

5

RECONFIGURING RESEARCH SITES AS WORLDMAKING PRACTICES

The posthuman 'vignettes' in this book demanded attention. We noticed them early on, entangling themselves in our meetings as a way to tell stories with multiple narratives that re-emerge across and beyond the book through intra-connected webs of meaning.

First sighting

As we enter the three-storey building for a home visit, feet thundering down two flights of stairs create a loud and exciting echo of movement and anticipation in the narrow corridor space. Eshal appears first, her sister Kabila behind her, and then Rihana, their mother. The two girls' dancing bodies lead us into their modest flat. It has one bedroom with a small, open-plan kitchen and lounge. Joanne sits on the couch (Figure 5.1). Sensations of care and love permeate the home. This is a place of living–learning relationships where conventional teaching materials like pencils, worksheets, and number cards fit in snugly with other furniture.

DOI: 10.4324/9781003205036-5

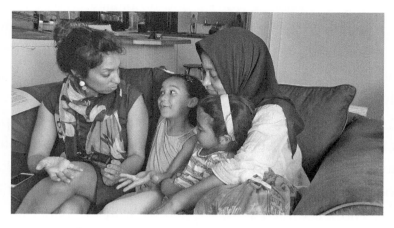

FIGURE 5.1   Sights on the couch

Rihana, Eshal, and Kabila settle in alongside Joanne. She relaxes into their closeness, welcomed by their bodies on the couch. The couch acts as a wall between the kitchen, lounge and the tiny bathroom. The couch feels big at times, too big for the games that are played on the carpet and the toys lying around that need more space to be enjoyed for their human-designed purpose. A trampoline leans up against the wall and begs the couch to be moved so that it can be jumped on. The couch isn't actually a disturbance for the trampoline, Joanne discovers, when she and Rihana address some of the questions in the parent interview regarding play. Rihana explains that she carries the trampoline down the two flights of stairs as the two girls follow behind carrying baskets of washing to be hung out in the sun at the back of the building. The trampoline keeps the girls busy while Rihana hangs up the washing.

In this vignette, we remember encountering Eshal in her home for the first in a series of four home visits. The performativity of thundering feet, dancing bodies, and hospitality enfolded in the couch set the scene for this chapter. Re-turning to the home visit with Eshal, her flat, toys, trampoline, GoPro, and picture books aerate the usual questions about what constitutes a 'research site'. In this chapter we open up and multiply the concept of 'research site', moving away from Newtonian conceptions of time and space that rely on binary logic (e.g., inside/outside, macro/micro, nature/ culture) (see Chapters 1 and 3). Drawing on posthumanist relational ontologies we continue to re-think conventional notions of time, space, and place (Barad, 2007). Staying with the performativity of these home visits is an act of de-composing with the data and becoming more deliberate as a way of reconfiguring the assumptions of what a research site 'is'. In thinking relationally with the data we trouble the bounded notion of research sites, continuing with cascading questions and concepts in this book.

In reconfiguring the concept of 'research site' we keep asking 'What is already given ontologically?' and 'What is assumed to be true (*a priori*) about research sites as fixed positions in space and time? What meanings influence what counts as 'home' or 'visit' or 'site' or 'play', or 'digital' when conducting research? Thinking relationally, we put to work Haraway's (2016) concept of 'worlding' (Chapter 2) as a way of noticing how things come to be in the world, and are of the world, in order to open and multiply the concept of 'research site'. Diffracting through Ingold's (2015) philosophy of lines enables a tracing of lines that disrupts bounded and fixed ideas of what constitutes research sites and that offers other ways of thinking about time, space, and land. Furthermore, we take up and think with research sites as a phenomenon (see Chapter 3). Thinking with and diffracting through multispecies relations, the 'whale' and haunted shorelines in Chapter 3, the melting bompie in Chapter 4, salty sea waters and a camouflaged octopus, we draw attention to relational entanglements of research.

In our agential realist account, postdigital play can be seen to come into being differently depending on the permutations and combinations of the particular "agentially intra-acting 'components'" (Barad, 2007, p. 309). Weaving one unfolding transmodal vignette through this chapter we are part of playful tracings of a lively meshwork of relations that come into being through human and more-than-human intra-actions (including octopus, tidal pool, sea star, sand, wind, WhatsApps, the local library, data, research sites, and researchers).

'Research sites' in research

Moving slowly in order to do justice to reconfiguring 'research sites', we tunnel through texts and compositions of research sites in order to open them up (Chapter 1). We slow down with the concept of 'research site'. We wonder how research sites are presented in texts on qualitative research methodologies that novice researchers are likely to consult. We are aware that there are a number of seminal texts (evident by the proliferation of new updated editions) that introduce students to research and to which experienced researchers tend to return. As we search recommended lists online[1] and find a number of them in our university libraries, we are struck by the common design features and layouts which remind us of textbooks.

Staying with only a few texts that could be considered to be seminal, four methodology text(book)s call our attention. We are interested in how visible the concept 'research site' is and what is written about it. These books shape how novice researchers learn 'how to do research' and furthermore consolidate existing research practices. We enter through the contents page and index of four text(book)s: We engage with Bhattacharya's (2008) entry on 'research site' in *The SAGE encyclopedia of qualitative research methods*; Cohen, Manion, and Morrison's (2017) *Research methods in education*; Merriam and Tisdell's (2015) *Qualitative research: A guide to design and implementation*; Creswell's (2020) *Educational Research: planning, conducting, and evaluating quantitative and qualitative research*. The discoveries are surprising.

As we search, we find that two of the texts, Merriam and Tisdale's (2015) *Qualitative research: a guide to design and implementation* and Cohen, Manion, and Morrison's (2017) *Research methods in education*, have no specific references to research sites in the contents page or index at all. Within the chapters, Merriam and Tisdale (2015) refer to participants being *located* in contexts in an off-hand way as if space is a container and not deeply implicated in the exercise of power (see Foucault, 2002). In an appendix, they provide a template for writing the methodology chapter which is where a discussion of research site/s would traditionally be placed. But is not. Their template has no mention of research site at all.

There is also no reference to research site in the contents page of Creswell's (2020) *Educational research: planning, conducting, and evaluating quantitative and qualitative research*. Research setting/context is mentioned only three times in the index. By following these references into the body of the text(book), we discover that research site is, in fact, not the focus. Rather, a research site is related to making decisions about sample sizes. The other two page references take us to paragraphs relating the concept of research site to ethnographic and narrative research, with research sites again mentioned in general terms that imply a taken-for-grantedness.

We are not arguing that all publications on research methodology do not consider the ontological complexity of the notion of research sites. We are interested in what novice researchers may find when they pull these text(book)s off physical or virtual library shelves. Why do 'research sites' disappear in these books, which, although not always explicitly written as textbooks, are nevertheless used as such? For us, this lack of visibility is dangerous and speaks to the ways in which places and spaces are framed as apolitical. In contrast, this chapter is a diffractive move through theorists such as Henri Levebvre (1991), Michel Foucault (1997, 2002), and critical geographer Doreen Massey (2005). Massey (2005, p. 10) argues that "space does not exist prior to identities/entities and their relations. More generally, I would argue that identities/entities, the relations 'between' them, and the spatiality which is a part of them, are all co-constitutive."

The fact that sites are invisible as a separate topic in the literature, points to a human-centric notion that space/site is unproblematic—a pre-existing place where researchers go to collect data. We argue that when research sites are conceptualised in this way, ingrained assumptions are reinforced: that research sites pre-exist ontologically *as* research sites. The lack of visibility in the literature speaks to their normalisation. However, not all researchers take the concept of 'research site' simply as a given.

In *The SAGE encyclopedia of qualitative research methods*, research site appears in a one-page entry dedicated to research settings. Bhattacharya (2008) opens up the concept by drawing on postcolonial theory. In her theorising, a 'research site' is not just a geographical place, demarcated by physical boundaries, it can also be a social group, everyday lives or bodies. Work such as this opens up opportunities to trouble the naturalness of a site, the human-centric notion that whole cultures can be contained and bounded by sites (see Gupta & Ferguson, 1997; Blomberg & Karasti, 2013) and challenges macro–micro dichotomies (Marcus, 1998). Posthumanism reminds us to think beyond the culture/nature binary and to notice the ways in which this binary sets up nature as awaiting cultural intervention by humans to produce meaning (Lien & Pálsson, 2021). Thinking with the postdigital (Chapter 2) further shifts considerations of sites as we consider the fluidity of movement between online and offline intra-actions, which includes tracing beyond the human and the complex quantum entanglements[2] across spaces rather than just humans (Dicks et al., 2005). We are re-minded of the performativity of the thunderous sounds, echoes, salty ocean sedimentations, and movement during the home visit with Eshal. We re-turn to the home visit in the next section to keep opening up more considerations about this concept of 'research site'.

Moving towards in/determinate 'research sites'

As outlined in Chapter 1, three research sites were identified in the research design for CTAP: home, school, and the site of a community activity. The research sites were clearly demarcated spatially and temporally bounded by the sequential organisation of three distinct phases of data collection. The home visits required a series of four to five visits that would allow researchers to interview parents and children, conduct activities related to technology usage and play, and observe the ten focus children in their family settings. During the school visits, researchers spent time observing the participating focus children in their classrooms, interviewing their teachers and conducting focus group activities with the case study children and their peers. The third site was defined as a community site, a place which children visit after school or on weekends. Suggested research sites in the project design that would count as a community activity were scout groups, religious gatherings, and sports activities. The purpose of the community visit was to experience the child in the community and interview the community member who led the activity. Figure 5.2 illustrates the three sites of the project for Eshal and her family. The school is on the left, Eshal's home is in the middle, and the local library, a community space that Eshal visited weekly, is on the right.

This ordering of home, then school, then community visit is not neutral, but political. It is underpinned by a particular logic and by assumptions about research relationships (Murris & Peers, 2022). In their article 'No Small Matter' critiquing Newtonian space and time, Barad (2017, G108) problematises "a nested notion of scale (neighbourhood $\subset$ city $\subset$ state $\subset$ nation) with each larger region presuming to encompass the other, like Russian dolls." It separates child from 'her' context.

In agential realism, these 'nesting' relations are not understood as geometrical, but as intra-actively produced through one another

FIGURE 5.2   Three sites: school, home, and the library

(Barad, 2007, p. 246). In other words, in this study, matters of scale come into sight where home is nested in school which is nested in the community, as researchers move from micro relations of the family to broader social relations. But, what are the possibilities when we think of research site as a phenomenon—an ontological move away from individual bodies first who are then in relation with one another? (see Chapter 3). Posthumanism troubles notions of unilinear time, that 'nesting' frameworks presuppose (Murris, 2022a, p. 15).

Thinking about research sites from an agential realist per-spective involves unlearning how we *see* space and place. Our lenses *matter*. In Barad's (2007) posthumanist account, sites and bodies are in/determinate, entangled, and extend ontologically across different spaces and a multiplicity of times. The entan-gled and fluid relations mean that research sites only become distinguishable as determinately bounded through *agential cuts* (Barad & Gandorfer, 2021; see Chapter 1). As we argued with play in Chapter 2, all the 'parts', in this case of a research site are mutually co-constitutive - the more-than-human is the con-dition of the possibility of human's existence. A nesting frame-work for conceptualising research sites (e.g., micro, meso, macro)—like CTAP's research design—takes *separability* as its ontological starting point: it presumes there is a Subject (child) that exists apart from its environment or surroundings (see Chapter 3). Considering this 'apparatus' (see below) we re-turn to the home visits to complexify the concept of research site. We show the ways in which the interview schedules in their material-discursive form and our own presence as research-ers are part of the worlding and boundary-making practices of Eshal's home as research site.

Following the lines of be-coming 'research site'

What is articulated throughout this book is that research designs and instruments are part of the world researchers are researching. The Baradian notions of quantum entanglement and phenomena trouble binaries at their core. Barad's diffractive engagement with quantum physics provides empirical evidence for reworking the notion of entanglement as *quantum* entanglement.

> Quantum entanglements are not the intertwining of two (or more) states/entities/events, but a calling into question of the very nature of twoness, and ultimately of one-ness as well. Duality, unity, multiplicity, being are undone. "Between" will never be the same. One is too few, two is too many.
>
> *(Barad, 2014, p. 178)*

Research designs and research instruments are not *applied to*, but ontologically *part of* the world of children, their play, their toys, and their families. As with the research methodology books mentioned previously, the construction and use of research instruments implicate them in what knowledges are produced, entrenched, and normalised. We illustrate how the parent interview schedule is an apparatus, a boundary-making practice, separating what is made visible and what remains invisible.

Diffracting through Ingold's (2015) philosophy of lines we seek to weave in-visible lines into sight to disrupt the bounded and fixed 'nature' of what conventionally constitutes 'research sites', including drawing a line between the digital and the non-digital (see Chapter 2). According to Ingold (2011, 2015), lines are a part of everyday life and dynamic in their relation with the world and cannot be presumed to be contained in fixed forms. Thus lines resist the notions of fixity (e.g., perimeter, border), and direction (e.g., linear, horizontal, sequential) where the emphasis is rather on the doings of lines with the world, "a movement of becoming" (Ingold, 2011, p. 83). This movement of becoming "includes walking, weaving, observing, singing, storytelling, drawing and writing" (Ingold, 2015, p. 54).

We also do not draw a line between 'us', researchers, and 'them', the researched. Humans are also "composed of lines ... or rather, bundles of lines" (Deleuze & Guattari, 2014, p. 323). Deleuze & Guattari (2014, p. 323) see these bundles of lines as 'lines of becoming' and "lines of 'flight". Lines of becoming and lines of flight are the lines through which life is lived. They explain that a line of becoming:

> is not defined by the points it connects, or by the points that compose it; on the contrary, it passes between points, it comes up through the middle ... A becoming is neither one nor two, nor the relation of the two; it is the in-between, the ... line of flight ... running perpendicular to both.
>
> *(Deleuze & Guattari, 2014, p. 323)*

Barad (2007, p. 235) would probably argue that lines are agentic— they are *apparatuses*. Lines are doings. Locating points in time and space, and drawing lines to connect them has no place in agential realism (Barad, 2007). Phenomena are not made up of connectable points which exist prior to their relations, or what Ingold (2015) would refer to as a network. Reading Barad diffractively through Ingold, phenomena are made up of a meshwork of lines which have no beginnings or endings. A meshwork of relational lines (Ingold, 2015) does not move in one direction or in a sequence of unilinear time and space, but is in/determinate (Barad, 2007). It is impossible to track or pinpoint beginnings and endings because meshworks are made up of "radiating lines, with all sorts of tiny conduits leading to and fro" (Latour, 2005, p. 177).

What the diffractive exercise invites us to do is to trace the in/determinate lines of the concept of research site. It is only "through specific intra-actions that the boundaries and properties of the components of phenomena become determinate and that particular concepts ... become meaningful" (Barad, 2007, p. 139). In this case, the concept 'lines' and 'research site' are only meaningful because of the specific intra-actions we need to trace. Concepts are "particular material articulations of the world" (Barad, 2007, p. 139). The act of drawing lines is a material-discursive practice that produces an agential cut in-between 'subject' and 'object' (Barad, 2007, p. 140), in this case, between researcher and researched.

Diffractively intra-weaving the interview schedule, the interview transcript, Joanne's memories in the unfolding vignette we pay attention to the movements in-between words—stutterings, pauses, loaded silences, the unsaid—from the audio and video recordings. Diffracting disturbs the perception of the home as a Newtonian container, a physical space *in* linear time and space where researchers collect data. This conceptualisation of space excludes land as agentic (as part of the phenomenon—'*exteriority-within*' (Barad, 2007, p. 140).

Eshal and her sister sit on the floor drawing for the two researchers, Joanne and Luzia, who have asked them to complete an activity for this home visit. The crayons that the children are using are under and between Joanne and Rihana's feet as they sit on the couch with the research interview questions.

Joanne remembers the overwhelming weight of all the questions listed for one visit. She scans the first page of the parent interview schedule:

- What are the parent/s' ages?
- Are they employed, and if so, what do they do?
- At what age did the parent/s leave school?
- What is their highest qualification? …

Joanne stops. Frowning with the text on the page she awkwardly rephrases:

Joanne: **Um, and** schooling-wise? I know you said you've been living here for now, but your own schooling?

Rihana (Eshal's mother): Where I …?

Joanne: Where did you … **ja**.

Rihana: Um, I went up to matric [Grade 12]. I failed my matric, that was in 1989.

Joanne: Ok.

Rihana: Mathematics and Biology. In 2008, I rewrote that subjects.

Joanne's body shuffles on the couch as the awkwardness grows. The interview schedule asks:

- Do the parents own a car?

Joanne: [stuttering] So, travel and transport-wise, **do you, do you** drive, or (pause)?

Rihana: No I don't drive …

Joanne: Ok.

Rihana: I'd love to drive but I'm too nervous of it. Uh, we used to walk to school but when winter comes, come with, came with the taxi. Or sometimes we

> get a lift from Mrs L, one of the teachers, she stays
> in Fish Hoek.

- What are the parent/s' ages?

Joanne: *Ok so I just wanna catch up with some of the ques-*
tions that I missed out the last time, and then ask
you a few more, if that's OK? ... [she looks down
at the interview schedule] Ok. **Um ... Oh***, it's on*
the, on the other section [pages rustle]. But it, **uh***,*
I needed to ask you the question about your age.
[laughs] **Sorry***.*

Rihana: *No, no, don't say sorry [laughs]. ... I'm 47.*

Joanne: *47? Ok. ...And her dad?*

Rihana: *Her dad is 69.*

Why did Joanne not ask the questions as they appeared in the interview schedule? The questions grew longer with stutters, shuffles, pauses, and heavy gazes in-between Joanne and Rihana instead of staying short and concise. It seems simple to ask "At what age did you leave school?" or "What is your highest qualification?" The transcript appears disfluent with Joanne relying on Rihana to fill in the gaps of her incomplete and incoherent questions. This could be read as an unprepared or inexperienced researcher trying to read unfamiliar questions in an interview. However, these awkward phrasings and pauses reflect so much more.

Rather than starting with the researcher's performance, we stay with the questions on the rustling pages of the interview schedule. In following the questions instead of using them to categorise and compare parents, the stuttering, fumbling, and pauses become something different. We become more attuned to how these questions are not neutral, they are political. 'Where did you go to school?' 'When did you finish school?' and 'What qualifications do you have?' are not innocent in the ways in which they capture information about the human condition. They are located in demographic categories that are constructed lines and connecting points.

These questions are entangled with lifeworlds in the global south and hook into the traumatic geopolitical and spatial realities of living in post-Apartheid South Africa (see Chapters 3 and 4). Time and space fold through the pauses and fumbling moments on the couch. We follow temporal and spatial entangling lines of what is visible and invisible, spoken and unspoken. On this couch, in South Africa, these questions vibrate with colonialism, slavery, Apartheid, and patriarchal religious practices. The couch, the home, and the country are not nested locations.

Schooling and qualifications are deeply interwoven with bodily memory for Rihana and Joanne. The pauses in the interview are not empty but full of voluminous lines of spacetimemattering. These pauses vibrating through the ums ("*Um, and schooling-wise?*" "*Um I went up to Matric*"), hanging in the incomplete questions ("*Where I … ?*" "*Where did you … ja*"), stretching OKs are thick with haunted agentic memories as relating lines of schooling and living move in-between Rihana and Joanne.

Diffracting through Walter Benjamin's "thick-now" (Barad, 2017c), we learn with Barad that memory does not work *between* moments in space but *across* times. When we so-called 'go back in time', we don't jump back into the past. Interestingly, in agential realism 'lines' are entangled multiplicities. In the 'thick-now of the present moment', times bleed through one another as quantum entanglements. Diffractively reading the past through the present in the 'thick-now' reveals the potential for justice (Murris, 2022a)—not by pinning hopes on some utopian future, but by rupturing the continuum of time and bringing the energetics of the past into the present and the present into the past (Barad 2017, pp. 21–23). Important for our vignette in this chapter are the implications of 'thick-now' for subjectivity, for notions of self-identity that are tied up with chronological time, and for the memories that intuitively seem to belong to 'me', the subject.

When Joanne says *"Um, and schooling-wise? I know you said you've been living here for now, but your own schooling?"* the thick now of the present pulls the past of the 'here' of Muizenburg as well as 'there' of the past, and the site of Rihana and Joanne's schooling. These historical events are not left in the past but threaded through the present intra-actions with the couch.

The history of Apartheid in South Africa which legalised the exclusion of people of colour from education reverberates as these two women sit on this couch in Muizenberg. Rihana, Joanne, and their families were not allowed to live in Muizenberg or attend school there. Muizenburg was a suburb demarcated for people racially classified as white. Rihana and Joanne's presence in the suburb would have been illegal and a crime. Muizenberg is not just a suburb, separated from the past, contained and defined by spatial geography; it holds the haunted memory of inequitable resourcing, infrastructure, and access for particular bodies to the exclusion of others.

The question about leaving school in the interview schedule implies that leaving is a choice and that schooling happens over an uninterrupted period of time. However, that is not the case when countries are, for example, at war, or face other political challenges. In South Africa, schools for people of colour were sites of conflict during Apartheid. School communities actively resisted forms of knowledge and acts of erasure through racialised curricula. During the 1970s and 1980s, there were extended school closures for people of colour and violent raids on schools. Time slips into the folds of the couch as the years and dates of schooling arise in disorderly arrangements. The textures of loss, violence, and effacement of school time for Rihana and Joanne are embedded in their childhoods. Rihana's skin and Joanne's skin tell stories of shared histories of schooling. The thickened presence of erasures, exclusion, and violence is sedimented by Joanne's reply of "OK" when Rihana tells her she failed her final year of schooling.

The pauses that echo in-between Joanne and Rihana are haunted by the figure of the 'ghost truck' of 1985 and intertwined with the Greek story of the Trojan Horse.

The South African Trojan Horse massacre took place in Joanne's and Rihana's neighbourhood in the Cape Flats. The pauses in the interview fill with haunted matter through a diffractive timeline where schooling and Apartheid intertwine. The diffractive storying, alive in the postdigital moment, is a temporal-spatial multiplicity with Tuesday, October 15, 1985.

On this day, an Apartheid police task force deployed a decoy truck to a suburb on the Cape Flats. A truck painted orange stacked high with wooden crates, first appeared to be a fruit delivery truck to the groups of school children from three of the neighbouring schools. Camouflaged beneath the wooden crates, the task force, armed with guns, emerged as the truck entered the middle of the crowd of schoolchildren and opened fire. (See the CBS Evening News report from 2013 entitled 'South Africa's deadly Trojan Horse' that tells a story of this massacre https://www.youtube.com/watch?v=KnWu4lAKDj0.)

1980s

What had happened in Athlone was the Apartheid norm, particularly at the height of the struggle in the 1980s. But what made that fateful day in Athlone different was that it was all caught on camera. (*Bernardo, 2020*)

1989

Rihana: Um, I went up to matric [Grade 12]. I failed my matric, that was in 1989.

1985

Jonathan Classen's guardian Charmaine Zulu: The policemen there were very rude to me. They asked me:

> "Who are you coming for?" and I said: "I'm coming for Jonathan Classen because I'd heard he was shot." The policeman said to me "The pig has died because of throwing stones. Do you agree with me Boesman?" So I replied: "Sir I don't know. I was not present when he was shot." They made me sign a paper that said I could collect the body and that only 50 people were allowed at the funeral. We identified him at the morgue. He had bullet holes in his chest.
>
> (*Bernardo, 2020*)

2020

Martha Evans: That footage is totally unambiguous … It is unambiguously, indiscriminate firing into a crowd of mainly schoolchildren without serious provocation. (*Bernardo, 2020*)

2005

Michael's Miranda's mother Georgina Williams: When we were in court for the inquest, it was like we had done wrong. The Boere looked at us like we were the culprits, like we were armed and dangerous and were going to attack them. We were so scared of them. It was only after the Truth and Reconciliation Commission that I stopped taking medication. I have kept Michael's marbles and the stone all these years. (*Bernardo, 2020*)

2008

Rihana: Mathematics and Biology. In 2008, I rewrote that subjects.

2020

To this day nobody has been charged with murder. (*Bernardo, 2020*)

Following the multi-directional flows of time through the rest of the transcript, we notice how Rihana moves through her memories, recalling how she benefited from post-Apartheid service delivery protests (similar to the protests in Henry's community mentioned in Chapter 3). The disruption these protests caused resulted in schooling being made available for high school children on Saturdays. These classes afforded her the opportunity to return to school and complete her schooling in her twenties in 2008.

These haunted stories pull Joanne into the past. She visualises the familiar school hall on the Cape Flats where Rihana wrote her matric examinations alongside teenagers in 2008, and the pavement where the school children gathered, and the ghost truck, and the primary school a few roads away where she herself sat in a classroom in 1985. Home as 'research site' multiplies as schools flood in and join with Rihana and Joanne on and with the couch.

Following the 'doings' of the interview questions is not an argument for not asking participants questions in research. Questions are important and provide insights into families. Thinking with lines of becoming in this chapter is a 'doing of justice' for thinking about research sites and research questions. The gathering of Rihana's relations with political, historical, geographical, educational, and patriarchal forces seep through the apartment walls de-composing the boundaries that keep the world at a distance.

Playful worlding with 'research sites'

In this section, we follow unruly lines with-in multispecies relations that came into being during the home visits with Eshal that take the research 'off script'. For Haraway (2016) there is something about our everyday engagements with other kinds of creatures that open new kinds of possibilities for relating and understanding the world. Haraway (2014) sees the world as a verb where the world is made up of doings and becomings-with as world-making practices. Staying with these performative lines is a decolonising move, a different way of becoming-with each other, of telling other stories (Haraway, 2016, p. 3). It is important that we notice the finer threads, the unfamiliar lines, the unexpected complexities in the meshworks of the world where human and more-than-human *relata* come to be in the world. These lines matter in their specificity, and following them is a matter not just of epistemology but ethics. This thinking generates leaky places (Neimanis, 2017) where ontologically, agency moves away from individual human bodies and research sites as physically contained and bounded in spacetime (see Chapter 6).

As researchers we are implicated in the practices of research, how we observe, what we look for, the tools we use to analyse data, what we compare, contrast, include, and leave out. We take account of how we affect and are affected with-in the home visits. Tracing the loose threads that fall outside the boundaries of the demarcated research activities enables a thickening of the concept of 'research site'. Importantly, for this chapter thinking differently about research sites is a reworlding practice—an "integral part of mattering otherwise" (Barad, in Barad & Gandorfer, 2021, p. 18).

The coffee table holds the spines and pages of a pile of library books which Eshal reaches for during the conversation. The books are piled untidily, they lean precariously but Eshal's hand confirms that she knows each book in the pile. Her fingers move to the exact place in the line of spines and draw out an Afrikaans picturebook, Seekat [Octopus]. *Joanne is not sure who is more excited, Eshal or her. A familiarity grabs hold of Joanne like a memory of the lyrics of a song which creates a feeling of comfort and expectancy. The movements of bodies and pages are fluid, Eshal and Kabila's bodies settle in against Joanne's in an age-old ritualised posture for sharing stories. The couch absorbs the flood of reminders of unexpected moments when books, pages, families, homes and children come together.*

> Eshal: *One, two, three… four, four fishes here!*
> Joanne: *What do you think?*
> Eshal: *Look what he can cook?*
> Joanne: *Well, look at how many things he is able to do, with all his tentacles.*
> Eshal: *And he has, he has a heart in his chest… a brain.*

FIGURE 5.3 Moving sights

The Seekat picture book, becomes a wild 'dis/connected' line that disrupted the scheduled activities for the home visit. Bodies tangle and fingers respond to the pages of Seekat as its tendrils draw Eshal, Kabila, and Joanne further into the tentacular storying (Figure 5.3). Our meeting with the Seekat octopus moves the research beyond the places demarcated by the original research design. Seekat-as-more-than-picturebook, or Seekat in the Baradian sense, is an apparatus that lures in an unexpected site, the nearby tidal pool. This more-than-fictitious octopus puts out a line to the octopuses dwelling in the tidal pool:

> Joanne: ... *I love this book! Because it's so, telling stories and it's giving facts.*
>
> Joanne: *Here we go. Sy is baie slim, sy het a groot brein in haar kop, en 'n mini-brein in elke arm.* [She is very clever, she has a big brain in her head and a small brain in each arm/tentacle.]
>
> Eshal: *You see?*

Joanne: *I never knew that. I want to take a photograph of that, 'cause that blows my mind.*

Rihana: *[Laughs.] Yes, 'cause the octopus are very smart, yes.*

Joanne: *I know! 'Cause I was going to say, do you think they are very clever, now that they have so many brains?*

Rihana: *I believe so 'cause I put the documentary of them on the TV.*

Joanne: *Yes, I love octopus. Do you, do you go to St. James ever? … the tidal pool?*

Rihana: *… not really.*

Joanne: *Not really? Did you know that, in that tidal pool, it's painted on the wall there, that there's an octopus living in …*

Eshal: *[Gasps] There's an octopus living in there?*

Joanne: *Yup.*

Eshal: *A real octopus?*

Joanne: *Yes, in the tidal pool … The next time I go, I … I'm probably going to go swim on Sunday, and I'll take a photograph.*

Eshal: *Of the octopus?*

Joanne: *I'll take a photograph of the wall, [Reading from Seekat] Groete uit die oseaan [greetings from the ocean] … Wow.*

The interview schedules rest on the arm of the couch. The lines being intertwined through the words, unexpected questions, laughter, and enthusiasm escape the research plan. Stories of swimming, water, and octopus become part of the ongoing multispecies world-making. World-making is a matter of "patterings, risky co-makings, speculative fabulations" (Haraway, 2016, p. 14). As we stay with the flows of the vignette, we encounter the ways in which worlds are made through risky and generative relations. These flows enable thinking differently about what comes to matter in research. The past seeps into the present as Seekat opens the research to unbounded ontological and place relations.

We draw attention to the assumptions that researchers make through their intra-actions with families. Although she phrases it as a question, Joanne assumes the family have seen the mural of the octopus at St James' tidal pool because it is a one-kilometre walk down the road. The assumption is entangled with their home which is situated at the iconic surf spot, Surfers Corner[3]. Implicit in this assumption is that proximity to a beach means that the family swims. Rihana doesn't swim. Eshal doesn't swim. Kabila doesn't swim.

Shefer and Bozalek (2022, p. 27) tell us that "as moving bodies of water, oceans are powerfully related to human and more-than-human stories across spaces and times, of power and subjugation, gains and losses, freedom and enslavement." The swimming stories float in the hauntings of the history of Apartheid in South Africa. The Apartheid state drew lines in the water—legislating which bodies could swim where. Thinking relationally, this is absurd—where does the land end and the ocean begin, and which water 'belongs' to which human bodies when it is constantly in motion?

Swimming becomes a performative act of disrupting the land and ocean divide. Swimming reminds us that where research happens is not in the 'place'. Research itself is a form of swimming, a practice of moving with the flows of the world, enfolding continuous movements, multiple ways of being and becoming-with the world. These flows include conversations with families in their homes, a process of becoming-with where lives and relations are shared. Joanne speaks about her own swimming, living close to the ocean for the first time in her life and learning to swim in the tidal pool. Rihana shares her fear of swimming and multiple attempts to overcome her fears through swimming lessons. However, despite this fear, she invites swimming back into the home visits.

> Rihana: *Did you go swim on Sunday, Miss Peers? 'Cause it was so cold …*
> Joanne: *Yes! It was lovely.*
> Rihana: *No, no, no, [laughs] it was so cold. It was raining the whole time.*
> Joanne: *No it only rained later, I went at sunrise.*

These conversations remind us how research practices work in material-discursive ways that set up boundaries in the professional relations between researcher and researched. Staying with this data asks us to think about the ways in which research is not a process where researchers take information given by participants without considering how this coming together affects the world. Swimming is a becoming-with through shared pasts and shared vulnerabilities (van Dooren & Rose, 2016, p. 87).

The GoPro is pulled into the meshworks, submerging playfully with the world. Inspired by Seekat, Eshal suggests that Joanne take the GoPro into the water when she next swims to find and record the octopus. The GoPro, conceived in the project as a device for families to use to collect data in the home to 'capture' play, intertwines with Eshal, researcher, and other creatures with-in the tidal pool. The GoPro becomes a lively line collapsing the boundaries between research sites, data creation, and analysis as it enables a tidal pool as another research site.

Joanne is drawn into the ocean in a different way with a GoPro. After a swim in the tidal pool, she shares the recording and photographs on a WhatsApp group with Eshal and her family. The South African research team had set up WhatsApp groups for parents and families to share examples of their digital play and experimentations with the GoPro. The WhatsApp group becomes a playful postdigital site where texts, emojis, video, photographs, and voice notes extend beyond its purpose as a data repository. The unfolding spacetimemattering with-in the vignette make visible the worlding intra-actions in-between child, octopus, and researcher (see Figure 5.4).

Playful postdigital worldings

Eshal catches the watery threads of the world where pools leak and join in response to other watery places and surfaces. Voice notes on the WhatsApp group are part of ongoing postdigital worlding. The world is made up of multiple lines and relations: spatial boundaries collapse as the micro (tidal pool water) intertwines with the macro (planet, oceans); places move through shared downloads saved on mobile phones; digital play keeps rupturing chronological time through digital practices. The research activities demarcated to home visits travel beyond the perceived perimeter of the four visits set out in the research design, be-coming unruly worldings.

We re-play Eshal's voice notes. The multiple voice notes in-between Eshal, Rihana, and Joanne and two smartphones (see Figure 5.5) amplify an unfolding of ideas and theories about the world.

Colours, earth, water, globe, and land are "part of the world and the reworlding of the world, in particular ways and not others"

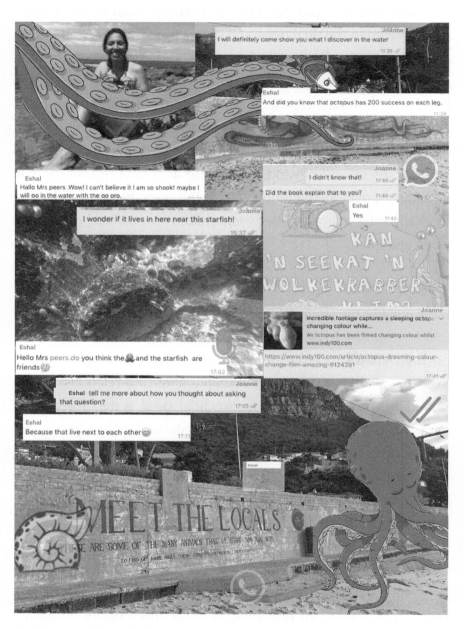

FIGURE 5.4 Virtual sights

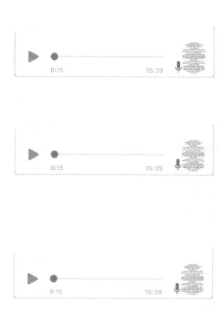

Eshal: Oceans and the seas
Eshal: Google say the planets look- look, look
*   what?*
Rihana: Looks green.
Eshal: Looks green and what again?
Rihana: Because of the land.

Eshal: Because of the land
Rihana: But it looks more blue actually.
Eshal: It looks more blue actually.
Eshal: Because there is more water on
*   the planet*
Rihana: Yes

Joanne: Hi Eshal! Do you think that that
*   information is correct? That the blue is*
*   from 70% of the water that comes from*
*   the oceans and the seas? That's a lot, hey.*
*   Don't you think?*
Eshal: Mrs Peers, we do have a lot of seas...in
*   South Africa. On the planet I meant*
Rihana: We have a small globe here.
Eshal: We have a small little globe here Mrs
*   Peers.*
Eshal: It looks blue when you look at it.

FIGURE 5.5   Multiple voices making worlds

(Barad & Gandorfer, 2021, p. 18). Becoming lines moving to and fro through WhatsApp, Google, books, and the globe are all part of Eshal's being and becoming with the world. With WhatsApp and postdigital worlding the pile of library books on the coffee table where Seekat resides grows as Eshal re-turns to the library in search of more books to explore land and ocean stories. These voice notes remind us that sites cannot be separated, contained, or nested in each other, nor do they have universally applicable and stable perimeters that perform in the same way in other phenomena and call for ways of researching differently.

Staying with multiple worldings

When we think of 'research sites' as phenomena, an entanglement of in/determinite relations rather than as separate bounded entities, we notice how things come into being in the world. In the preceding section, we have shown how sites are multiple and always already part of the world. In this section, we discuss how another site comes into being through playworlding with Seekat. Putting out a line, we re-turn to Chapter 2, where playworlding is the movement in-between being and becoming, having no discrete identity (being) other than as a characteristic of an unbounded event, the ontological difference produced through encounter (becoming). Eshal keeps de-stabilising the ontological assumptions of 'research site' as a bounded place located in time and space as she follows relational lines with Seekat, earth, and water. Joanne, Heloisa, and Luzia find themselves co-inhabiting the library through the voice notes and then later with Eshal.

The local library is inseparable from the entangled relations as it weaves through the WhatsApp group, coffee table, and GoPro (Figure 5.6). Instead of being a predetermined, pre-planned site for the community visit, the library becomes part of the meshwork of vibrant relations. There is no need for the researchers to arrange a visit with the librarians. Eshal folds the library, library books, and librarians into the world in-between home visits. She co-creates

Eshal: *Good evening Mrs Peers. It's me Eshal. How are you today?*
So today I went to the library and took the GoPro with and they took a video of me in the library. Uh-uh, a video of me in the library and they also took of the libra-libra-rian. Li-bra- It's hard to pronounce it. Li-bra-rain, li-bra...
Rihana: *-rians, librarians*
Eshal: *Uh librarians and I, went there to go get my books. So, I took a video of it.*
Rihana: *I made a video...*

FIGURE 5.6   In another voice note

FIGURE 5.7 Multiple watery worlds

research sites by introducing the research project to the librarians and prompts us to visit the library as a communing-with.

Eshal moves us away from the perceived separation of the digital, play, and learning. Sitting with library books, Eshal invites the tidal pool to the table (see Figure 5.7). The submerged playful swimming-with underwater GoPro, brings ocean sounds, voices, and re-searching into the visit. Watery tidal pool sounds and salty ocean smells blend with dusty library books and the swish of pages turning. Fluid relational spaces are generated. Ingold's (2015) exploration of oceanic worlds, where tendrils and tentacles weave an ever-extending meshwork through octopus and anemone relations resonate with-in the library. Ingold elaborates on the interweaving of bodies (e.g., octopus and anemone) where bundles of lines are fluid and escape the attempts to locate them in an enclosed site (e.g., picture book, octopus den, tidal pool). We notice other crafty forms of escape recorded by the GoPro that were initially missed by the swimming human eye:

Eshal: Is this where you met the octopus? Is this where you found the octopus?

Joanne: This is when I came across that tunnel that I showed you.

Eshal: I asked you ...I asked you, was it in the wall?

Joanne: It was against the wall, that gap yes.

Eshal: But there it is white! It is white!

Joanne: You're right Eshal! I did not even see that.

Eshal: So the octopus does live there.

Rihana: It lives in that hole.

Eshal: Right, it does live there. Right?

Joanne: I think we might be on it.

Eshal: Okay, stop. You have to go up a bit. You see now it is staying still. So you can't see it.

Joanne: It is camouflaged.

Eshal: Yeah, it was camouflaged that's why you couldn't see it.

Rihana: Like they say in the book.

Joanne: What did they say in the book?

Eshal: It changes colour, so it was camouflaged, to the colour of this wall. You could not see it because it was brown.

Joanne: Oh, I see.

Eshal: You didn't see it?

Eshal: Maybe there is like a thing where water can come out there then the octopus can protect it.

Joanne: Protect it? The water or ...

Eshal: The water from going out.

Joanne: So, who is he protecting? The water?

Eshal: *The other animals, like the starfish! Maybe it's protecting him because the water doesn't want to come out. That's why.*

Eshal: *I asked you, are they friends?*

Joanne: *I was very …*

Eshal: *There's a starfish!*

Joanne: *I was very unsure if they are friends, but I wondered if you just lived next to something if you are then friends?*

What does it mean to live together? What is friendship? Haraway (2010, p. 2) responds to the questions with more questions:

> Who lives and who dies, and how, in this kinship rather than that one? What shape is this kinship, where and whom do its lines connect and disconnect, and so what? What must be cut and what must be tied if multispecies flourishing on earth, including human and other-than-human beings in kinship, are to have a chance?
>
> (Haraway, 2016, p. 2)

Octopus, libraries, starfish, WhatsApp, couches, Seekat, participants, and research are not entities alongside one another but joined together through space and time in and with the world (Figure 5.8). The continuous camouflage and mystery of an octopus which appears on Eshal's coffee table, on the wall of a tidal pool, in a GoPro, between the covers of Seekat, inside a computer screen on the library table does not settle for one place or moment in time. In fact, it opens up possibilities for multispecies flourishing with space and research in the thick present. Taking response-ability for this way, rather than that

FIGURE 5.8 Multispecies world-making

way, is not an after-thought, as it often is in research (Bozalek et al., 2021), but is part of worlding. Thinking response-ably moves away from human-centric thinking where humans alone can respond. World as a verb renders water, land, more-than-human species capable of responding, furthermore as co-constituters of the world (van Dooren & Rose, 2016).

Un-ending worldings

What comes into being when we attune beyond the human to how research sites, as phenomena, co-create data related to postdigital play from this project? Slowing down with the couch we resist answering the question (see Figure 5.9). As if swimming, we drift with the making and thinking-with of 'research sites'. We linger

FIGURE 5.9   Unending sites of worlding

with 'research site' as more-than-physical, un-ending, becoming-with-out borders and unilinear sequences.

Eshal as more-than-focus-child thirsts for worlding with the world. She invites us as researchers to see the world as an ongoing process of becoming, co-authoring new ways of diluting pre-determined boundaries created by research designs and research practices. She pushes us out of the constraints of dominant forms of knowledge circulating in well-worn research tomes. Taking into account that research sites are inseparable from the world enables doing global education research differently. Research is richer, thicker, playful, constantly on the move in an un-ending becoming with the world, made visible through

   storymaking,
        weaving,
            playing,
                swimming,

reading,

recording,

voice-noting,

entangling.

Notes

1 We looked at sites like: the PhD Assistance (2019) blog, https://www .phdassistance.com/blog/what-are-some-good-books-on-research -methodology/; Collin's (2023) recommendations on the Become a Writer Today site, https://becomeawritertoday.com/best-research -books/ and Lifehack Laboratories' (2023) recommendations on https://bookauthority.org/books/best-educational-research-books

2 The notion of quantum entanglement is further elaborated on.

3 https://www.surfers-corner.co.za/

6

RECONFIGURING AGENCY AND CREATIVITY IN YOUNG CHILDREN'S POSTDIGITAL PLAY

Agency and phenomena(l) agency

The arguments put forward in Chapters 2 and 3 show how in dominant tropes of western thought, child agency tends to be attributed to a being (an individual body) with the capacity to act. In the World of Subjects (Chapter 3), action is conceptualised in a narrow sense and in terms of *intentionality*: the agent's mind, that is, mental states, conscious intentions, reasons, and events *cause* the body to act. These human-centred conceptualisations of agency are made possible by the Mind/body dualism (see Chapter 1). They shape dominant research theories and practices in the social sciences, humanities, and law and are embedded in developmental children's rights discourses.

Moreover, this human-centred perspective informed the CTAP research design and analysis. Children are understood as 'having' agency. It is a quality they possess and something they can have more or less of. Intricately related to the notion of agency is the idea that a child has a 'voice'—a voice that needs to be listened to. Creativity is also discursively framed as a valued enactment

DOI: 10.4324/9781003205036-6

of individual agency. As discussed in Chapter 2, the researchers working on the CTAP project used the LEGO Foundation's
Learning through Play Experience Tool (LtPET) for analysis of data
(Marsh et al., 2020). In this chapter, we re-turn to the LtPET tool
and discuss how it works to perpetuate humanist notions of child
agency.

For posthumanists, notions such as 'voice', 'agency', and 'intentionality' are no longer *in* individual subjects as knowers and thinkers.
Nor are they only produced through social or cultural means (among
humans). This is still an unusual perspective of human beings' agency.
It raises challenging questions: surely, attributing voice and agency to
individual children through, for example, children's rights discourses,
is empowering? Are hard-won gains of autonomy at risk of being lost
perhaps?

Some possible answers and some provocative propositions
come into view for us as we write. Two vignettes in this chapter render both child-human and the more-than-human capable (Despret, 2004; Haraway, 2016). We read and write with the
vignettes re-cognising how the intra-active nature of agency works
in postdigital play research—as the mutual constitution of entangled agencies that can, but might not, involve humans. Such a
move, Barad (2013, p. 17) argues, is "not a mere exercise in metaphysics, or physics," on the contrary, "what is at stake are questions of justice and response-ability." The vignettes also put our
own subjectivity as storytellers at risk. We trouble our agency, our
beliefs about intentionality, intelligence, choice, free will, and indi-
viduality—critical markers of what it means to be (Adult) human
and sedimented markers in research involving children. Our stories chip away at the very concretised foundations of the Culture/
nature divide that has made it possible for the Adult human to

keep the 'other' at a distance: child, animal, inanimate objects. They touch on the metaphysical prejudices about ourselves and our place in the world that are (unfortunately) written in our bones. The ontological distancing many of us Adult humans are so good at, is doing some serious damage to 'other' humans and to the environment—a world 'we' humans are a part of (Giorza, 2021).

In Chapter 1, we stated that various analyses of specks of CTAP data would give a flavour of what it is like for *phenomena* to be agentic (and not individual beings-human or not). For Barad (2007, p. 352), the concept 'human' does not refer to individual things (objects) with inherent properties in the world, for example, with agency or with "the ability to engage in cognitive functions that make the universe intelligible." Importantly, the posthumanist move to *decentre* the human does not *erase* the (child)human (Murris & Osgood, 2022). On the contrary, as we have seen through all other vignettes so far, although posthumanism rejects oversimplified and non-relational notions of the human as *a priori*, they involve an ontological re-working of relationality. And it is done in such a way that, ironically, by *emphasising* the important role the more-than-human plays in agency, the collaborative role of *human* agency, creativity, and voice in research is amplified (Murris & Peers, 2022).

The vignettes in this chapter are agentic in the sense that they show how our postqualitative re-turning to the data invites a different 'art of noticing' (Tsing, 2015), of becoming affected by phenomena and sensing the material-discursive connections rather than focusing on individual bodies, whether human or more-than-human. They also trouble the research instruments we use (and that use us) to measure agency, creativity, and progress in (post-digital) play.

Intricately connected to the way in which we theorise play and agency, 'creativity' is also understood as transindividual. Creativity is not a quality possessed by an individual human who has creative capacities, but is distributed and includes the more-than-human, such as technology, land, wind, atmosphere, sound, smell, colour, national curricula, international benchmark testing, etc. Rather, it is a force or energy that emerges as new and unexpected links, connections, relations, and effects are produced. Through detailed material-discursive analyses of video clips, audio recordings, and transcripts of various focus children of the CTAP project, we return to the concepts 'postdevelopmental', and 'postdigital'. We make a case for reading children's play differently.

This chapter involves 'unzipping' the (child) human body as we enquire more closely into the ontologies some common conceptualisations assume and who and what is excluded by them. This reconfiguring move is key to decolonising play and the notion of postdigital play that will continue to unfold in this chapter.

Reconfiguring play as postdevelopmental: Zuko takes a picture

Plastic bricks are becoming-truck in the hands of Zuko at play on the classroom floor. Luzia and her smartphone camera observe Zuko during one of the scheduled school visits. Zuko gazes at the camera and Luzia. The truck morphs into camera, as Zuko's literate fingers respond to Luzia's analytic gaze. The camera spies the smartphone and the smartphone spies back. Pictures taking pictures of each other. Luzia's and Zuko's spontaneous laughter reverberates and sound waves connect through this playful event. Luzia is aware that as the watching researcher she is being watched.

Responding to this vignette, we discuss how humanist notions of child agency are illustrated by the LtPET tool-as-apparatus (see Table 6.1). The LtPET tool aims "to see a play experience through the eyes of a child and use[s] this to understand the texture of the child's experience" (van Beeck, 2020, p. 3). An introduction document[1] for the LtPET tool cautions that, "[t]he tool is not designed to rate or evaluate the individual child, but to understand how adults can better empower and enable children's experiences" (LEGO Foundation, 2020, p. 1). Originally developed for play involving LEGO bricks (in the LEGO House in Billund, Denmark), and specifically designed taking into account the cultural settings of Australia and the United States, the tool is intended to glean generalisable and more broadly applicable information about the child's or children's play to be used in planning and offering new play opportunities.

The *child's* perspective, however, is obviously central, as all of the descriptions are written as 'I'…statements (e.g., "I feel a sense of accomplishment," "I play collaboratively with others"). Describing the LtPET tool, we write in the CTAP report:

> The tool begins with an analysis of how far a playful experience is agentic. When children have agency, they are active in making choices about their play and have a sense of self-efficacy in relation to their play experiences. The psychological scaffolding of the LtPET consists of the six stages of agency: Non-Play, Passive, Responding, Exploring, Owning, Transferring.
>
> Non-play is when a child shows no interest in an activity. If a child has a minimum sense of agency, she or he will simply follow the instructions and be in the Passive stage. The next stage, Responding, is when the child responds to the design

TABLE 6.1 Learning through Play Experience Tool (LtPET) used in the CTAP project (From: Marsh et al.2020, p. 6)

State of Play	Joyful	Actively Engaging	Iterative	Meaningful	Socially Interactive
Non-Play *I am opting out of the experience*					
Passive *I am following instructions*	I am neutral about the experience	I am following the play or instructions of others	I do not know how to respond to this experience	I am doing this because I have to	I am alone or in a group not by choice
Exploring *I am considering possibilities*	I am curious about the experience	I am interested in the environment and materials	I interact with the experience	I attend to the experience	I am aware of others
Owning *I am choosing my own path*	I am enjoying the process, even if it is challenging	I am focussed on the activity	I adjust my approach	I am developing my understanding	I play with others or let others approach me
Recognising *I have new insights*	I feel a sense of accomplishment	I am invested	I am deliberate about the changes I make	I show how the experience is relevant to me	I play with others collaboratively
Transferring *After the experience I am reflecting on how this experience can influence the reality of my own life, and have confidence that it changes myself and others*	I am enthusiastic about trying this again	I have tried this again after the experience	I seek out and explore new projects	I recall the experience and use it to understand other things	I cooperate with others to initiate new play experiences

elements, a welcoming parent, peer, or facilitator and begins to form intentions. If the child's interest is piqued, she enters the Exploring stage and begins to explore different elements and set her own goals. Then, if the play experience reaches a high level of quality, the child enters the Owning stage where the experience and learnings are internalised. Finally, with play experiences of the highest quality, the child becomes able to transfer the learning to other situations; this is what is meant by playful experiences of the highest quality. The Transferring stage can only happen after the playful experience in question.

(Marsh et al., 2020, p. 196)

The quality of a play experience is based on five play characteristics, defined by the LEGO Foundation as "meaningful,"' "actively engaged," "iterative," "socially interactive," and "joyful" (drawing on Zosh et al., 2017). Each, in turn, helps assess the quality of the child's play experience as an indication of learning taking place and moreover what is required in terms of adult mediation to improve the learning experience. The influence of the material, technology, and context on learning through play is also assessed, but importantly, no differentiation is made in the LtPET tool between physical and digital technologies. The tool is developmental in that what is assumed is that by moving down the stages of agency, high-quality play experiences lead to deeper learning.

The LtPET tool draws on Albert Bandura's concept of agency. Bandura is well-known for his self-efficacy and Social Cognitive Theory (SCT). Inspired by a Darwinian non-teleological notion of development, Bandura (2008, p. 15) proposes that humans are unique in that language and abstract thought has made cognitive agency possible; "transcending the dictates of their immediate environment." He argues that humans' "advanced symbolizing capacity" has given them the power to shape their environment and override environmental influences (Bandura, 2008, p. 15). Agency so conceived positions the human (knowing) subject as separate from, and 'transcending' its environment and relations with other humans and more-than-humans. Bandura (2008, p. 18) continues that a child is born with no sense of self and needs to learn through observation, imitation, and modelling. What is critical here, is that Bandura's humanist notion of child agency is already at play in the LtPET, that is, given—even before the research starts. What is assumed is that children develop their autonomy by increasingly acting independently (the normative underpinning goal of the instrument) and by becoming more con-fident in learning new things and by making their own choices.

Using the LtPET to analyse the play event, Zuko's play can be seen to be of the "highest quality" (Marsh et al., 2020, p. 196). In terms of the state of play, Zuko appears to be Exploring, Owning, and Recognising (we cannot assume Transferring happens across all categories as this would require durational data collection). The laughter with Luzia indicates a Joyfulness with a possible "sense of accomplishment." He is Actively Engaging and appears invested in the play event.

The play is Iterative and Meaningful because Zuko deliberately makes changes to how bricks are supposed to be used, asserting his autonomous decision-making agency ("I am deliberate about the changes I make"). He is symbolically taking on the role of the adult researcher, enacting an internalisation of the modelling that is central to self-efficacy. The play is Socially Interactive. Zuko is not just mim-icking adults around him but independently creating meaning in play and initiating a collaborative play experience ("I cooperate with others to initiate new play experiences"). In the World of Subjects lens (Chapter 3), sees Zuko holding a camera made out of plastic bricks that are passive and inert (Figure 6.1). It is Zuko's individual intentional actions and competencies that have turned the bricks into a 'camera'. The sedimented humanist conceptions of agency and play are affirmed in this reading.

In Chapter 2 we asked if the LtPET taxonomy could be diffracted through in a way that would allow the agency of the material and the co-productive power of collaborative engagement between and among the human and non-human to be recognised. Staying with and applying the LtPET tool from a *postdevelopmental* perspective, we reach an impasse. Observing and analysing 'the' child assumes individual performances and representational practices

FIGURE 6.1   Zuko taking a picture of Luzia

of trying to match the measuring tool with what is happening in reality, evaluating a child's performance. Performativity from an agential realist perspective does not necessarily imply human agency. In contrast, posthumanist performativity is nonrepresentational and not human-centred. It troubles the anthropocentrism of the still dominant research practices in the humanities and social sciences when assigning meaning to visual evidence such as body position or facial expression.

Playing with agency

We stay with the blurry edges of the vignette[2] that bleed outwards and incorporate into the phenomenon (this 'agential cut'), more stories about Zuko's ways with bricks in the classroom and at home.[3] We follow the lines of the stories that the research produces: an interview with Zuko's mother, Carla, and father, Alex; a question raised by theorist, Maggie MacLure, about our adult role; and the ethical challenges presented by the consumerist toy industry.

> Carla: *We normally try and encourage him, the first time he opened the kit, it's been kits that have instructions. We got one of those kits that are just creative LEGO and they got some ideas in there, multiple ways that you use the same blocks. Yeah, but the other kits he's been given, like mostly presents and stuff and then you have like a specific thing that you follow the instructions and build.*
>
> Joanne: *Okay.*
>
> Carla: *Like I say, he can do that, but he doesn't love to do that. He's like, 'Can't I just do my own thing?' Yeah,*

> *that's kind of his usual orientation with learning, is,*
> *'Let me make my own thing, let me try it myself,*
> *why do I have to follow instructions?'*

Joanne: *And then does he engage with other LEGO port-*
folio things like films or things on Netflix or other
branded things to do with LEGO?

Alex: *Are you going to ask about Dad's LEGO?*

Joanne: *Ah, no I think you've asked yourself about Dad's*
LEGO.

Alex: *Well Zuko is not allowed to play with Dad's LEGO.*

Joanne: *Okay, yet.*

Alex: *Yes, yet, I have (said), when he's a bit bigger, then*
he can.

In the interview Carla talks about Zuko's resistance to follow the manufacturer's building instructions of the LEGO kits he receives as presents. What becomes clear is that he likes to do his "own thing." Clear boundaries are set by the parents between what Zuko is allowed or not allowed to do. The insistence on following instructions is perhaps indicative of the adults' own adherence to fixed notions of learning and knowledge and their own constrained ways of playing.

According to Deleuzian childhood scholar, MacLure (2016, p. 176), adults routinely discipline "a bit of the world" for children through exercises "in grammaticality and representation." Through the use of fixed definitions of concepts as embedded within a research design (and in the LtPET in this case), adults tend to "pin … meaning to the body of the world and the body of oneself" by investing actions "with purpose and reason," establishing "what is normal and meaningful" (MacLure, 2016, p. 176).

MacLure (2016, p. 176) comments that in this way children are not only taught their place within this represented world by thinking "in terms of the fixed relations of similarity and difference afforded by the logic of representation," but also they learn that "it is possible to stand 'outside' this world to observe and comment on it." In the normative developmental process of growing up into so-called mature adults in control of their emotions and thinking rationally and scientifically about the world through binary logic (Murris, 2016), children are also disciplined to occupy a "view from nowhere" (Haraway, 1988). Quoting Deleuze and Guatarri's (1980/2014) *A Thousand Plateaus* (ATP), MacLure points out the significance of this representational logic for agency:

> [Children] are thus invited to occupy the position of the "central point" or "third eye" which, according to the "law of arborescence," ranges over all space, dispensing binary oppositions: "male-(female), Adult-(child), white-(black, yellow, or red); rational-(animal)" (ATP, p. 292). This central point that surveys all and dispenses binary oppositions, while installing itself as the principal term of each opposition, constitutes the majority. Even when exercised by women (as here), or children or people of other ethnicities, the majority is coded male: It is the exercise of a "virile majoritarian agency" (ATP, p. 293).
>
> *(MacLure, 2016, p. 176)*

MacLure notes that no agency or personal responsibility is assigned to the Adults[4] involved in these disciplinary practices, either at home, in school, or as part of a research project. Although speaking from a majoritarian position, adults too are subjected to the very same disciplinary practices because there are no such things as individual statements; all roles and identities "are drawn from the assemblage that precedes and envelops [them], and which confers subjectivity and social obligation" (MacLure, 2016, p. 176). Zuko's father, Alex, has clear ideas about when it will be appropriate for Zuko to be allowed to play with 'his' LEGO. In this way, children (all humans in fact) are colonised into embracing a notion of agency that performs an individualised notion of masculine subjectivity—"the majority is coded male" (above quote). This non-relational subjectivity involves the internalisation of the logic that has made colonial superiority and the notion of the ontological 'other' possible.

Othering involves treating 'others' *as children*, in the way in which, for example, Africa as a continent can be treated as a child, that is, in need of development (Murris & Reynolds, 2018). The logic of childhood places Adults above nature and is used to justify the colonisation of land, natural resources, and children. In contrast, the posthumanist *relational* conception of child agency disrupts the idea that childhood is always and only, temporally and spatially located *in* a child and characteristic of a young human being of a particular age.

Kohan (2015) offers a postdevelopmental, non-chronological relationship between child and time. Like Deleuze, he draws on Heraclitus' concept of *aion*. Kohan reconfigures childhood as an *experience* of a specific strength, force, or intensity and dislodges the concept from necessarily being connected to a period in a human life. The figure of the Deleuzian child, although "inextricably bound up with the materiality of the child's body and its relation to language" (MacLure, 2016, p. 173), isn't about chronological child on its linear path towards Adulthood. As a-grammatical artisan, child causes "language to stutter" (MacLure, 2016, p. 176). MacLure (2016, p. 176) explains:

Not yet fully striated by the rules of grammar that order and subjugate the world, children challenge "the hegemony of the signifier" (ATP, p. 15) by remaining open to multiple semiotic connections that do not obey the laws of conventional language and representation.

Unhinged from chronological child, posthumanist analyses decentre the human and shift the attention from individual agency to the even more complex agency of the historical, material, linguistic, political, environmental, and socio-economic 'contexts'. Although Zuko's, Carla's, Alex's, Luzia's, Joanne's agency matters, agency is not something *in* the children (or *in* the adults), or a quality they *possess* but of the phenomenon they are part of relationally. In the absence of a better word, the use of 'contexts' does not do justice to the fact that bodies (both human and non-human) do not exist separately from their environment or surroundings. In a World of Phenomena (Chapter 3), bodies and environment are inseparable and are the conditions for each other's existence.

The distinction between the epistemological and the ontological is often unclear, but appreciating how they are related, and work differently, and why this matters (scientifically and ethically) is key to understanding the current paradigm shift in postqualitative research practices. As MacLure would put it, for research to be postdevelopmental it needs to acknowledge and mobilise its a-grammatical tendencies, its own "becoming-child" (MacLure, 2016, p. 180). So, returning to the Zuko vignette, we need to switch optics and read it as a phenomenon that is agentic. (For a much more detailed analysis, see Murris, 2022a, 2022b.) The human and more-than-human (e.g., concepts, land, building, plastic, phone, curriculum documents, LtPET, research questions,

research funding, teacher, pedagogies, parents, Zuko, researchers) and different temporalities are always already shot through
the 'now-moment'[5] when a play event occurs (Barad, 2017c). In
the 'now', time is diffracted through itself: past, present, and future
enfold through one another in a non-unilinear manner (Barad,
2010, 2017c). Matter, Barad argues (2007, p. 118) is the sedimenting historicity of practices/agencies and an agentive force in the
world's differential becoming. Importantly this also includes symbolic readings, but not as something that happens *in* the mind.
Meaning-making is always already a specific material doing or
enactment of the world in its iterative becoming. In that sense,
play is *a worlding process.*

Diffraction as methodology (Murris & Bozalek, 2019a), discussed in Chapter 1, disrupts more 'obvious' representational
descriptions. The vignette is neither a purely factual or neutral
'capturing' of the play event, nor is the vignette as data a representation of what happened independently from the researcher's gaze. Analysing data diffractively involves installing oneself
in an event of 'becoming-with' the data (Haraway, 2008, p. 16).
It involves not uncovering the (symbolic) meaning *behind* the
vignette in a representational way but as *a separate, newly unfolding event*—different from what actually happened in the home
or school or when the play event unfolded. Transcripts, vignettes,
or visual (still or moving) images do not enable researchers to go
back in (unilinear) time and analyse what was 'really going on',
in or with the child, but are 'new' material-discursive events, and
emerge only as 'new' events with the reading of the data (Murris
& Menning, 2019; Chapter 3). Researchers are also entangled with
the phenomenon, activated by the vignette in its becoming data.

Readers, like yourself/ves, engaging with this text become part of new phenomena.

Moreover, such iterative and diffractive engagement through 'the' data not only involves cognition, but also a be(com)ing affected by the experiences of bodies in relation. With a posthumanist analysis the very constitution of matter—the photo, the smartphone taking the photo, the plastic bricks, Zuko, the researcher's writing—are not objects or things, but phenomena(l), so always already entangled in less-than, more-than, and other-than-human relations. In that sense, like all matter, plastic bricks are political. Tracing the infinite entanglements transdisciplinary exposes the limitations and the political implications of only using the dominant socio-cultural lens in education research (the World of Subjects[6]) and opens up possibilities for the 'other' to respond (e.g., plastic bricks, smartphone, land, mining of tantalum, tin, tungsten, gold, and cobalt in digital devices). Objects, including the technology used to create the data (smartphones, GoPros, etc.), are materialised (e.g., economic) practices, gendered (Osgood, 2019) and "congealed labor" (Barad in Juelskjær et al., 2021, p. 138). For example, LEGO bricks' material durability is an asset (for humans) and an integral part of the design, and indeed has inspired a wide variety of aesthetic expressions, but its durability is also an environmental curse.[7] These toys that middle-class children can afford are produced mainly by cheap labour elsewhere (China, Mexico). As expressed by Barad, (2007, p. 393):

> We (but not only "we humans") are always already responsible to others with whom or which we are entangled, not through conscious intent but through the various ontological entanglements that materiality entails. What is on the other side of the agential

cut is not separate from us – agential separability is not individuation. Ethics is therefore not about right response to a radically exterior/ized other, but about responsibility and accountability for the lively relationalities of becoming of which we are a part.

As discussed in Chapter 2, Harker (2005) suggests that we need to resist trying to pin down what play *is* by giving definitions. Instead, he suggests we need to write, "alongside playing as difference, without trying to inhabit it" (Harker, 2005, p. 53). This powerful gesture towards taking age out of play (Haynes & Murris, 2019) is an ontological turn towards reconfiguring play as material-discursive and postdevelopmental and meaning as 'post-verbal'. As Zuko turns the camera towards us and plays with our Adult gaze, the photo's agency as part of a phenomenon brings about the urgency to reconfigure digital play and agency as relational. The transindividual analysis of Zuko shifts the focus from intentionality and child-human skills and competencies in digital play to the politics of the material-discursive network of relations of which both child-human and plastic bricks are a part. This is essential for reimagining more equitable futures, especially in resource-constrained environments. Western notions of agency are at odds with the current drive to decolonise education research.

Reconfiguring play as creative 'intensity': becoming-with the bling of the world

Digital worlds live on the material pages of a research diary that Della has filled with drawings (Figure 6.2). Inked lines coalesce to form a body of a winner. Eva Marie, a wrestler in the WWE franchise and Della's WWE Smackdown avatar, stands triumphantly glowing under a spotlight in the middle of a wrestling

FIGURE 6.2 Della's research diary page featuring Eva Marie's win

ring. Fingers grip her championship belt. Vibrant red hair and a red leather costume contrast with high black knee-length boots. The atmosphere is charged. Love and hate words fly. A thought bubble holds malevolent secrets. This victory is not unanimously supported. Posters of Eva and her opponent are held aloft, flapping against the noise of the crowd. The body of her opponent lies prone and dazed, leeched of colour.

Drawing is a regular practice for Della, her twin brother Linton and her older sister Bongi. The children took to the research diaries enthusiastically, quickly filling all the pages with drawings about their play. In the CTAP research design, research diaries were used as a research tool, particularly with the 'younger' children (e.g., four- to six-year-olds) as a way to reflect on their play. But Bongi is an integral part of her siblings' playworlds and became an inseparable part of the research data. Once Theresa realised that the two girls had a collaborative intra-active playworlding practice she provided Bongi with a diary as well. Della and Bongi's drawings are inspired by the fashion and style of the young women wrestlers from WWE Smackdown they play on their PlayStation. Asymmetrical hairstyles and funky outfits including elbow-length gloves on their favourite personalities are drawn with precision. Linton, on the other hand, prefers super-hero and football-related video games, but enjoys watching his sisters play.

The diaries proved to be generative in "catalysing rich research conversations about the children's conceptual engagement with their play practices" (Murris et al., 2022, p. 546). Re-turning to the diary pages sparked these conversations which importantly led us to an appreciation of the more-than-semantic content of the transcribed data (see also Chapter 4). Although language and conversation were an integral part of the collaborative play shared by the siblings and also of our home visit transcriptions, it is the sensory register that becomes significant and the affective energies that flow among the intra-active components of the research events.

Elizabeth de Freitas, whose work in the field of mathematics education is motivated by an interest in moving beyond representationalism and a human-centred cognitivist notion of learning, pays attention to the sensory, noting that: "sensations are a collective resonance of intensity—a resonance effected across a collective (of child-cube-ipad), rather than *by* an individual" (de Freitas in Juelskjaer et al., 2021, p. 88). 'Prosody' is the term de Freitas uses in her exploration into how affect and material entanglements animate pedagogical conversations (de Freitas in Juelskjaer et al., 2021). "Prosody helps by bracketing the semantic force of language and directing our attention to other forces that we share with other animals" (de Freitas in Juelskjaer et al., 2021, p. 82). Meaning-making, seen as a worlding practice, de-centres human language, cognition, and agency.

At the heart of Western notions of agency is the foundational dichotomy of autonomous, intentional human and passive nature. An agential realist reconfiguration of meaning-making and of agency disrupts both the individualism and the human-centredness of this conception. Re-turning to the WWE PlayStation bout explored in the cartoon comic sequence in Chapter 2, and reconfigured in the vignette incorporating Della's diary page that opens this section and continues through it, we show that creativity and agency are part of more-than-human phenomena rather than intentional human attributes or dispositions.

Being in and with the world as it 'worlds', can be a joyful and awe-inspiring experience if we allow its beauty to affect us. Theorising the concept 'shimmer' from a posthumanist perspective, Australia-based anthropologist and eco-feminist, Deborah Bird Rose has written about an aesthetic sensibility that goes beyond an anthropocentric experience, drawing from the wisdom of Aboriginal wildlife carers:

> The term bir'yun [translated from Yolngu as 'brilliant' or 'shimmering']—which does not distinguish between domains of nature and culture—is characteristic of a lively pulsating world, not a mechanistic one. Bir'yun shows us that the world is not composed of gears and cogs but of multifaceted, multispecies relations and pulses.
>
> *(Rose, 2017, p. 55)*

The 'relations and pulses' that Rose refers to emanate from animate and inanimate sources. This distributed joy-ful creative force coheres with the "thing power" that, according to Bennett, allocates agency across the divides of human/non-human; living/non-living. It recasts us humans as "vital materialities" (Bennett, 2010, p. 21), un-doing human exceptionalism and human-centred notions of agency and creativity.

Returning to and turning over the LtPET tool, joy as one of the characteristics of play is understood differently. Joy as a concept is used to track the increase in agency along its six-stage developmental trajectory for an individual child. The tool requires that joy is 'read' off the body, including emotions, and movements of the individual child playing. Although we also subscribe to including joy as part of the phenomena of play, we are troubled by the deployment of a humanist lens (see Chapter 3). We also recognise the connection between joy and the relational and material expression of creativity in play. Donna Haraway in an interview with Anna Tsing and Greg Mitman puts it eloquently when she says:

> Play is sustained by joy. Nobody is going to stay in a play bout unless it's sustained by joy. For one thing, it's too dangerous. Play is never safe. There's something about that that feels to me really fundamental to being an organism.
>
> *(Haraway, in Mitman, 2019, p. 19)*

As organisms, we humans share a capacity for joy. Can we conceive of joy as a more-than-human force that moves across environments of learning?

Haraway then refers to Rose's theorisation of 'shimmer' to expand on the connection between play and joy:

The things that we care about sustain us because of their bling. It's not all that hard to play. It's actually not all that hard to sustain joy if we let ourselves. Joy is not innocence; it is openness to caring … Really we live on an astonishing planet, and we may as well just let the astonishment in.

(Haraway, in Mitman, 2019, p. 19)

This vignette has no clear boundary, as it moves between and within Chapters 2 and 6 and in-between the concepts of play, fighting, creativity, the postdigital, researchers, participants, sites, and technologies. Play-as-intensity is a strong force field connecting human and more-than-human, material-discursive energies. We show how 'joy' can be reconfigured as a relational and more-than-human phenomenon. In the playworldings in the vignette (Eva Marie's win [Figure 6.2], and drawing the pearl glove [Figures 6.3, 6.4, and 6.5]), joy emerges as an intra-active intensity of connection between the children and sensory and sensual experience and spectacle.

Barad warns that emergence does not happen once and for all, as an event or as a process that takes place according to some external measure of space and time. Rather:

time and space, like matter and meaning, come into existence, are iteratively reconfigured through each intra-action, thereby making it impossible to differentiate in any absolute sense between creation and renewal, beginning and returning, continuity and discontinuity, here and there, past and future.

(Barad, 2007, p. ix)

FIGURE 6.3   Diary page showing multiple images including a hand

In other words, the reading of the data also already includes the research instruments (e.g., questions we ask, the diaries) the material-discursive apparatuses that draw lines (Chapter 5), include us as researchers analysing the data. These relata shift and change with each relational intra-action. Through the playful repurposing of the prescribed research tool, the young participants render, for example, the diary agentic as a new playtimespace. Intense disturbances to human exceptionalism and cognition-as-knowing are produced by the diffracting energies of digital play, drawing games, and creative production.

In Della's drawn re-creation of the play episode with Bongi (see Chapter 2), the crowd is made up of a majority of the opponents' fans, who boo the winner. The WWE Smackdown game is a ritualised performance featuring expert strutting and

FIGURE 6.4   Della drawing around her hand

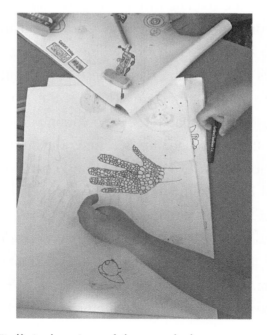

FIGURE 6.5   Della's drawing of the pearl glove

prancing and the crackling of heightened emotions and play fighting convincingly captured in Della's drawn renditions (which recasts Eva Marie as victorious even though she lost dramatically in her WWE Smackdown game to Bongi-Alexa Bliss).

In his book, *What animals teach us about politics*, Massumi (2014, p. 65) invites us to put humans on the "animal continuum." This requires the "mutual inclusion" of the "animal in the human and the human in the animal" (Massumi, 2014, p. 65). We share and exhibit animal attributes, and we are a member-species of the animal kingdom. Relooking at wrestling in the light of animal play fighting-as-learning gives a different perspective to the drama. The digital humanimals in the ring show an intense commitment to both the risk and the pleasure of the contest. Subtle body language plays an important role, as in any animal play encounter, and seasoned spectators are able to read the signals of play within the aggression of the performance (Massumi, 2014, p. 4).

The performance of 'animal' play practices—like prowling and pacing—are supported by costumes that enhance the intensity of their presence. The 'actual' Eva Marie is an actress who has a website with links to workout programmes and a line of women's sports fashion. Eva Marie, like all the female characters, has a very particular style and her outfits are an important feature of the spectacle that wrestling is. In the PlayStation bouts that we witness, Eva Marie sports a provocative full-length red leather coat with black feather trim. The exuberance and the feral qualities of the players' outfits inspire Della's fluent and prolific creativity.

Feathers have been an element in human adornment for millennia and more recently in commodified fashion. The fashion in 19th century Europe for feathers and stuffed birds on hats led to a number of species of birds becoming endangered (and in some cases totally extinct) and necessitated the passing of laws to stop the killing and importation of migratory birds to Britain and later to the US and Europe (Johnson, 2018). The lure of beautiful plumage is part of the same force of attraction that fashion and style exert. Victorian women in towering feathered hat constructions strutted the streets in emulation of avian courtship (ironically perhaps, most of the brightest plumes would have been garnered from male birds in mating season). Our increasing knowledge of the precarity of our earthly ecosystems brings a new awareness of the threat that extractive and exploitative overuse of such resources poses.

Fashion and profit have to be fiercely reigned in through international treaties and border controls, but we continue to borrow from other species to enhance our powers of attraction and visual impact. Creative use of colour, form, and movement are attributes we humans share with our more-than-human world.

Re-presentations and re-turnings on the diary pages compost the elements of fashion, style, texture, and colour to produce more and different permutations of possibility.

Pages of the research diary display drawings with areas coloured in with hatchings of felt tip and crayon. Above the turning pages float the excited, high tones of Della, Bongi and their brother, Linton who joins in with commentary and questions. Temporalities of gaming sessions, re-matches, re-tellings, and drawn reconstructions fold into one another. Personalities, avatars, their costumes and their signature music haunt the atmosphere. The performance spaces of living room, virtual wrestling ring, and diary pages flow into one another. Sparked by the traced hand on one of the pages that entrances Della's gaze (see Figure 6.4), hands reach for a pen and she invites us into a game.

Fingers and pen trace carefully around a small hand resting on the sheet of paper. "Just wait!" Della says. "You'll see." We patiently wait for her to complete the drawing (Figure 6.4). In gleeful anticipation of our response, Della proceeds to fill in the entire shape with small tightly packed circles.

"What is it?" we ask.

"You have to guess."

"Is it bubbles?"

"No."

"Is it sweets?"

"No."

… It's a pearl glove!

The pull of the pearls is contagious, and we are drawn into Della's worlding with iridescence and spherical diffractions of shimmery light and colour (Figure 6.5). Theresa asks which one of the WWE wrestlers wears a pearl glove. Della and Bongi are adamant that none of the wrestlers wear pearl gloves. This is Della's idea. Theresa searches the Internet to find out if perhaps Della is part of a larger pearl glove cult. Nothing comes up. As mentioned in Chapter 2, Alexa Bliss, another character in WWE, wears a silver skeleton glove. This 'glove' is more like a piece of jewellery, as it is made of silver metallic material and comprises tarsal bones with moveable links that mimic the bones under her skin. In a threatening prowl, Alexa Bliss challenges her opponent, wearing her skeleton on the outside. We are invited into Della's fascination with the potential of glove-ness.

Eventually we find an advertisement for some serious bling: a pair of silver velvet gloves adorned with pearls of different sizes. They are selling for US$425. We appreciate the joy of Della's multispecies 'fashion play'. But, with a sense of the precarity that haunts the splendour and beauty of the planet. The iridescence of pearls has captivated Della and inspired her invention.

We argued in Chapter 2 that it is impossible and pointless to attempt to track the boundaries between the digital and non-digital in children's play. Similarly, it is not helpful to track the movement of flow from one to the other. The two do not exist as discrete entities nor does one precede the other. Postdigital play is a worldly phenomenon that emerges agentially through co-configurations of becoming.

Marvelling at the treasures that the earth and its creatures produce (leather, feathers, and pearls for example) the wrestlers and the young players adorn their bodies and spar in playful multispecies imitation. The humanimal play extends beyond PlayStation and WWE. In an interview during another one of the home visits, the girls' father Martin describes the girls' long-established fascination with mermaids and their strong desire to wear and swim with a fish's tail.

> Theresa: So you were saying they talk about …
> Martin: Ja, they like, sort of like a mermaid.
> Theresa: A mermaid?
> Martin: Ja, Fin-Fun.
> Theresa: Fin-Fun.
> Martin: Ja, they call it Fin-Fun. I heard it from them. They like showing these pictures of mermaid dresses and

what-what. Normally they will imagine themselves as those mermaids.

Theresa: *And then they choose the outfits or something?*

Martin: *Yes, actually, I was forced to look. Actually I went around looking for that. Especially for the two [girls].*

Theresa: *Oh, you couldn't find the …*

Martin: *The pink mermaid dress. The one that she wanted.*

Theresa: *Oh, right, ja, ja! She talked to me about it.*

Martin: *Ja, I looked around, because I couldn't find it, because she desperately needed it.*

The vibrancy of matter (Bennett, 2010), the "bling of the living world" (Haraway, in Mitman, 2019, p. 19) and the "shimmer" (Rose, 2017, 2021) are animistic forces of human and non-human agency—that we claim pervade the girls' play. Their delight in fashion, beauty, the 'call' of materials (Bennet, 2010) like leather, feathers, pearls, and fish tails and the thrill of the embodied performative spectacle pervade the spacetimemattering of research diary production. The idea of knowing with "the sheer bling of life" (Haraway, in Mitman, 2019, p. 19) calls for an acknowledgement of the lively and compelling beauty of our pluriverse and its place in knowledge-making. Learning, conceived as part of an agential realist becoming, is "a rhythmic folding of sensation, a modulating intensity that traverses the tactile surface of our material entanglements" (de Freitas in Juelskjaer et al., 2021, p. 88).

Play and precarity: postdigital worldings

Things we care about and are drawn to include all kinds of living and non-living entities. These are our 'kin' according to Haraway (2016) and the bonds that tie us together are the affective connections that charge the world with meaning. Postdigital play is one of the foremost engines of meaning and mattering for young children in the contemporary world and as such merits our focussed attention and enquiry. This chapter has endeavoured to explore the meaning of creativity and agency in relation to post-digital play and it has done this through presenting, from a post-humanist perspective, co-created data from the CTAP research.

The vignette featuring Zuko and the plastic bricks offers an opportunity for readers to consider the postdevelopmental pos-sibilities of play. Child and play are recognised as concepts that defy limiting categorisations but that offer extensive and contin-gent differences in meaning and import depending on how they are performed in and with the world. Agency is not located within any individual nor is it confined to the realm of the human. The recognition of dynamic intra-active material-discursive relations allows for the tracing of co-response-ability for the state of things.

The second part of the chapter traces a deep engagement by child research participants with a globally marketed digital gaming product, drawing attention to the significance of play and creativ-ity as distributed multispecies phenomena. The joy experienced in taking part in the lively becoming of the world in its exquisite-ness is expressed through Della's diary. Beyond age and beyond spe-cies, play is an energetic force that pervades the world and is part of transindividual agency and creativity.

Inseparably bound up with our world in all its exquisite precar-ity, as (Adult) (human) researchers with a commitment to more just and equitable futures, we acknowledge and take up the task of becoming more attuned to the stutterings and the more-than-semantic messages shared with us by a multiplicity of human and more-than-human agents and creatives in our midst.

Notes

1 See https://learningthroughplay.com/learning-through-play-experience
   -tool where you can download the rubric, explanation, and guidance.
   The tool is regularly updated and evaluated by the LEGO Foundation.
2 See more about our theorising of vignette in Chapter 1.
3 For one such story, see Murris, 2022b.
4 As in Chapters 1 and 3, we use Adult with capital 'A' when we want
   to express explicitly how the concept 'Adult' creates a power producing binary between adult and child.
5 For more on 'now-time' and hauntology, see Chapter 5.
6 See Chapter 3 for the differences between World of Objects, World
   of Subjects, and World of Phenomena.
7 For example, see Baranuik (2023)'s article on LEGO's use of plastic.
   https://www.wired.co.uk/article/lego-haunted-by-its-own-plastic

7

TENTACULAR MOVES FOR POSTDIGITAL RESEARCH

The trestle tables: meeting the families

It is late 2023 and after long delays caused by COVID-19, the researchers, families, and children from the Children, Technology and Play (CTAP) project come together, including participants from two follow-up projects on digital play. The venue for this meeting is an old Victorian-style house that is home to an educational NGO. The meeting becomes a research fairground enacting early childhood pedagogies. The meeting is a 'gathering': bringing about unpredictable "happenings" (Tsing, 2015, p. 23). As Barad (2007, p. 353) eloquently puts it: "All real living is meeting. And each meeting matters." Meetings bring forth the world in its specificity, including ourselves and much of this book has been about the different ways in which we as researchers are accountable for our part(s) in the world's differential becoming through our practices.

In this chapter, we re-turn to previous chapters in this book and attune to the intricate details that matter ethically and politically in the notion of postdigital play and how it works (differently).

DOI: 10.4324/9781003205036-7

However, justice is not a state or an endpoint that can be achieved once and for all. This book does not offer final answers to the questions that drove our enquiries about (post)digital play. It does not offer a list of do's or don'ts. On the contrary:

> There is only the ongoing practice of being open and alive to each meeting, each intra action so that we might use our ability to respond, our responsibility, to help awaken, to breathe life into ever new possibilities for living justly. The world and its possibilities for becoming are remade in each meeting.
>
> *(Barad, 2007, p. x)*

But let's not get ahead of ourselves. Let's re-turn to the event we started with in this concluding chapter. It is Spring in Cape Town. The (extended) families are entering the building (with the spiders, ants, and other unloved ones). We meet a dad on his own, proudly recognising two of his children in a poster. One of us remarks how, as researchers, we occupy vastly different worlds. On the one hand, there is the academic world of research ethics committees, increasingly dominated by 'legalese'—a discourse that helps protect institutions from being sued. Then there is the world of children and parents with whom we have built strong relationships. Although close relations are necessary for co-creating data that matters, when disseminating the findings we need to guarantee anonymity. But the faceless images cause some disappointment among families looking to celebrate their and their children's involvement. The photographs were discretely taken so as not to reveal the identities of 'anonymised' participants, or we edited them afterwards.

After entry to the building, visitors (some from as far as the USA) are invited to rotate through different activities carefully set up in different 'corners' of the house. In the central meeting space, images from the research projects are strung up like bunting. It is in this room where children and their families are formally thanked for their participation. The atmosphere is playful, filled with laughter and warmth in and between human and more-than-human. The sun is shining. Without it being planned as such, the meeting starts and ends with choral singing as so often when people meet in South Africa (access the QR code diffracted through Figure 7.1).

One of the activities is to make connections between and beyond a selection of images from the data with the help of boards, string, pins, scissors, and concepts that swim around in digital play research (e.g., 'bossy-ngqongqo-baasspelerig', 'time-ixesha-tyd', 'angry-nomsindo-kwaad', 'imagination-imbono-verbeelding'). The words are printed in three languages of the Western Cape (English, isiXhosa, and Afrikaans). See Figure 7.2

FIGURE 7.1   Meeting families around the table

FIGURE 7.2   Making connections across, through, and beyond

Another activity is the *Mad Hatters Tea Party*, more usually known as *Speed dating*. Thought-provoking and fun questions about children, technology, and play are explored together for an hour in moving and rotating pairs, for example:

DO YOU AGREE WITH PARENTS WHO WORRY THAT PLAYING COMPUTER GAMES IS ADDICTIVE?

WHAT WOULD YOU RATHER BE AN IPAD OR A COMPUTER GAME?

IF YOU COULD BE A CHARACTER IN A COMPUTER GAME **FOR 24 HOURS**, WHICH ONE WOULD IT BE?

IF YOU COULD BE A CHARACTER IN A COMPUTER GAME **FOREVER** WHICH ONE WOULD IT BE?

IN WHAT WAY IS DIGITAL PLAY DIFFERENT FROM OTHER KINDS OF PLAY?

In another room, a panel of research participants perform a cyclical discussion on a video recording playing on a screen. Outside, a drawing station invites multi-generational mark-making with paper and pens and chalkboards and chalk. Snacks and drinks circulate. But some discomfort rumbles in our stomachs. What is this research all about, really? For whom, and for what, is it produced, we wonder. The world of research is so far removed from what seems to matter to research participants in the local communities.

Reconfiguring our role as researchers 'post'-COVID-19: dis/identification

Postqualitative research and ethics can't be pulled apart. As we have argued, to work with knowledge means to work with questions about existence. We are a part of what we are researching and as such are implicated and inseparable from its becoming (see especially 'World of Phenomena' in Chapter 3). So, what are the implications of our involvement in the CTAP research project and how we have storied 'the' story? Doing research postqualitatively requires a commitment to tracing the research relations (human and more-than-human) in all of their complexities, histories, geopolitical nuances, and lively contingencies. For example, in Chapter 5, octopus, libraries, starfish, WhatsApp, couches, Seekat, participants, and research are not entities alongside one another but joined together through space and time in and with the world (Figures 5.8 and 5.9). The continuous camouflage and mystery of an octopus which appears on Eshal's coffee table, on the wall of a tidal pool, in a GoPro, between the covers of Seekat, inside a computer screen on the library table does not settle for *one* place or moment in time. In fact, it opens up possibilities for multispecies living together in the thick present.

As touched upon in Chapter 1, postqualitative research responds to the ontological turn enacted by posthumanist philosophies. Posthumanist ontology is an "ongoing re-opening" (Barad & Gandorfer, 2021, p. 16) of reality from which we cannot remove ourselves. We are a part of, and implicated in, the ongoing becoming of the world. Ontology, therefore, is inseparable from concerns relating to knowledge and ethics. We are responsible, along with our co-constituting response-able others. The added hyphen in 'response-able' works in the following way:

> [It] indicates that the responsibility lies in researchers both making themselves susceptible and sensitive to different forms of response and in enabling a response, providing the phenomenon under study (of which the researcher is an enacted part) with the opportunity to respond.
>
> *(Barad in Juelskjær et al., 2021, p. 144)*

Meeting (the universe) and becoming-with means reciprocity and relationality. This means noticing, listening, sensing, and rendering one another capable of response (Bozalek, 2021).

Scientific objectivity is still possible, but only within particular circumstances, arrangements, phenomena, or 'agential cuts'. There is objectivity and "exteriority-within" an agential cut but a cut is not made from the outside, and not "once and for all" (Bozalek & Fullagar, 2022, p. 30). As Barad puts it:

Indeed, ethics cannot be about responding to the other as if the other is the radical outside to the self. Ethics is not a geometrical calculation; "others" are never very far from "us"; "they" and "we" are co-constituted and entangled through the very cuts "we" help to enact. Cuts cut "things" together and apart. Cuts are not enacted from the outside, nor are they ever enacted once and for all.

(Barad, 2007, pp. 178–179)

Ethics protocols can hide the fact that every step of research is relational and therefore all have ethical implications. Some university ethics committees are sensitive to the fact that changes are expected and inevitable, but the application forms can set up an assumption that once the ethics approval has been granted, then a green light has been given and the study can proceed along a pre-planned route. Research proposals and budgets have profound ethical implications and possibilities and are subject to all kinds of unexpected complexities, refusals, changes-of-mind, as we touched upon in Chapter 4. In their material-discursive performativities, ethics profoundly affect research practices and findings. In the CTAP research, the COVID-19 pandemic prevented any collaborations after the data collection phase of the research. The pandemic was part of the story of how the research unfolded and the reason for not being able to celebrate the publication of the report (Marsh et al., 2020) and the dissemination part of the research. At the same time, the COVID-19 phenomenon is a helpful example of illustrating how human-centred (and 'Human' of a particular kind, see Chapter 1) and objectifying Western thinking is.

The phenomenon of the research and our book writing are entangled with the pandemic and include relations with illness, viruses, and 'lockdowns'. For many people, the virus was and is an extraordinary danger outside 'us' humans to be eliminated and controlled. This was done, for instance, through disciplining bodies to comply with the demand to wear face masks, to sanitise hands, to physically distance, and to be isolated for quarantining, medical care, and even death. The virus is positioned *outside* the human and provokes the powerful questions: 'What does it tell about us human researchers and or relations with "others" that we view the virus and the world in this way?' and 'What are the dilemmas provoked when inhabiting a World of Phenomena, rather than a World of Subjects or a World of Objects (Chapter 3)?' Kerryn continues to live-with the after-effects or the (long) hauntings of a particular community of coronavirus microbes.

Individualised and human-centred notions of (self)identity tend to be taken for granted. Typical of working with a relational ontology in posthumanist research is the notion of 'dis/identification'. Instead of starting from identity, whether virus, university, ethics protocols, or human, even the smallest bit of matter is a multitude and traced (we mean: *dis/identified*) as a phenomenon. As we have illustrated throughout this book, all bodies (micro *and* macro) are unbounded by their skin, because each 'self' or 'individual' is already "made up of all possible histories of virtual intra-actions with all others" (Barad, 2019b, p. 542). There are no absolute insides or outsides in a relational ontology. For example, in Chapters 2, 5 and 6 playworlding is the movement in-between being and becoming, having no discrete identity (being) other than as a characteristic of an unbounded event. Ontological difference is produced through encounters (becoming) where GoPro, remote, referee, cables, and hands are entangled (see Figure 2.3). Eshal in Chapter 5 keeps de-stabilising the ontological assumptions of a 'research site' being a bounded place that is located in time and space as she follows relational lines with Seekat, earth, and water.

In the undoing of 'it' and 'self', the Derridean notion of hospitality is not only a human affair: "the 'other' is always already with-in" (Barad, 2019b, pp. 543–544). And this includes not only the human research participants, the other animals, the virus, the face mask, but also those already dead, and those not yet born. The posthumanist troubling of identity and here/there, now/then, inner/outer, human/matter binaries is expressed through Barad's diffractive 'forward slash' (Murris, 2022a). Dis/identification as a research strategy *matters* (politically) because it highlights who and what matters, and for whom. It makes normative, dominant discourses look strange and profoundly reconfigures what it means to be an object, a self, a human, a researcher, or a virus. At the same time, the '/' is a 'cutting together-apart'—an agential cut (see above) (Barad, 2014). Importantly, dis/identification does not introduce a binary or opposition between identification and disidentification but is a diffractive move. They are always already in dynamic relation.

Bound by the formal ethics clearance from the School of Education (University of Cape Town) and the Western Cape Education Authority—in and by itself part of the World of Subjects in its ontology—we faced and felt many ethical dilemmas. Our discomfort during the dissemination event is only one such example. The value parents ascribe to being able to see' their children-in-action as part of the research conflicted with the ethical requirements set by the university. These are built largely on medical research practices assuming a 'doing to' and are equally applied to social science and humanities research where human relationships are central and contingent (Lahman et al., 2015; Giorza, 2021). The assumptions underlying the expectations of guaranteeing anonymity and confidentiality in research have been explored by these and other scholars, problematising the assignment of pseudonyms by researchers with care and cultural sensitivity (Allen & Wiles, 2016).

Children were very aware of being researched and often turned a playful gaze back on the researchers. During one discussion about the allocation of pseudonyms as per the ethics agreement one of the focus children asked a researcher, "Will you also change *your* name?" The CTAP research team is immediately responsive to the sting of this question.[1] Another ethical question that stung was about the equitable allocation of GoPro cameras for children to use in their homes which we discuss in Chapter 3. These questions resonate with our concern for performing more ethical and response-able research. In Chapter 6, Zuko's action of building a camera of LEGO bricks and turning the lens to the adult researcher illustrates how "matter is political through and through" (Barad in Juelskjær et al., 2021, p. 138), but also foregrounds the binaries we routinely assume as given in education research, such as adult/child, human/matter, researcher/researched.

Swimming in an ontological tsunami and getting stung

The vignettes in this book give an imaginary of how and why large international research projects can be, and should be, designed differently, along *tentacular* rather than straight lines. In our performative re-turning as a research practice, we unsettle the Humanist subject—the cause of so much trouble. In that sense, posthumanism is an ontological tsunami and writing this book has felt like dipping our toes in, getting wet, swimming, and almost drowning in the complexities of doing justice to the richness of the CTAP data.

We re-turn to Donna Haraway and think-with her concept of the *Chthulucene* (Haraway, 2016) to shed another light on why this book matters. From *khthonios*, meaning in ancient Greek 'of the earth', *Chthulucene* is a way of resisting the term 'anthropocene' (Crutzen & Stoermer, 2000). From *anthropo* ('man'), and *cene* ('new'), this name has now settled itself as the common name to describe the geological time when human activity has left a permanent impact on the earth's climate and ecosystems. Haraway (2016, p. 30) points out that this naming practice itself, again, expresses human's self-invented exceptionalism, supremacy, and individualism. The centring of the 'human' has already caused enough trouble. Theresa Giorza (2021, p. 32) argues that Haraway's *Chthulucene* is a proposal—for something wilder and more poetic [than the *Anthropocene*] "(c)alling up the powers of the underworld and subterranean and other earthly creatures." Through a series of vignettes, this book traces the geopolitical dimensions of space, time, and the more-than-human. It asks profound questions of us researchers by disrupting the taken-for-grantedness of key concepts such as 'research site' (Chapter 5), 'data' (Chapters 1, 3, 5, 6), transcribing (Chapter 4), agency and creativity (Chapter 6).

The inclusion of South African land (and water) as more than merely 'background', or 'context', does justice to multiple temporalities and the more-than-human. It brings to the fore the importance of matters of scale that are 'normally' obscured from human vision. Scale profoundly affects who traces, and who or what is

included in the tracing or not. It matters which tracers trace traces
…. The vignettes of Eshal, Henry, Zuko, Della ripple on, and dis/
continue to affect readers, including ourselves. We diffract through
an interview between Martha Kenney and Donna Haraway drawing on the work of Eva Hayward with the sensory apparatuses of
the creatures of the coral reef. Donna Haraway lures us into touching, feeling, and stinging tentacularities:

Donna Haraway:	vision can be figured as touch, not distance, as entwined with, or negatively curving in loops and frills, not surveying from above. For a long time, since before I wrote "The Cyborg Manifesto" and certainly in "Situated Knowledges," I was interested in reclaiming visuality as a becoming-with or being-with, as opposed to surveying-from.
Martha Kenney:	… and also that wonderful word that I learned from Eva—*tentacularity*—the ways that figures, stories, multi-sensory appara-tuses reach out to their audience and enrol them …
Donna Haraway:	… and engulf them and sometimes *sting* them [laughter] because a lot of these tentacles have little poison sacks and darts on them; they are apparatuses of predation as well. These are not innocent figures; these are figures of living and dying, of risk and entanglement. These are figures for inhabiting attentively with response-ability.

(Davis & Turpin, 2015, p. 258; our italics)

Indeed our stories *"sting."* They *should* sting. They sting *us* too. Their poison alerts and propels us forward into a wilder, more poetic, and decolonising doing of educational research. Perhaps the most important lesson to take from our agential realist reading of the data is the ethico-political dimension of our research with children that is always already there, but often remains ignored or avoided. Researching with children is philosophically deeply complex in its human and more-than-human relationality. The political is part of the reality of the apparatus of postdigital research. Reconfiguring research with young children's play with technology involves an ontological tsunami. It is epistemologically unfamiliar for most Western-educated researchers, but ethically and politically of extreme urgency in the *Chthulucene.*

The stinging alerts us to the "thick now": the *Jetztzeit* (or 'now time' of Walter Benjamin) diffracted through the phenomenon of quantum erasures (Barad, 2017c, p. 21). The thick-now constitutes specific relational configurations that produce the becomings of the present with which pasts and futures are folded (Barad, 2017b). Reading Henry as a phenomenon in Chapter 3 includes the more-than-human as part of co-creating Henry's agency. The vignette illustrates how technology does not simply represent the past within the present but keeps time open as an ongoing worlding process and leaves traces by be(com)ing affected by the experiences of bodies always already in relation. Another example of stinging dis/comfort is the sticky bompie in Chapter 4. The historicity, time, space, memory, Afrikaaps, and the Cape Flats cannot be diluted in the more-than-apple juice bompie which joins the conversation about transcribing as a research practice.

In agential realism, the present is not one thin slice or a bead on the string of consecutive and chronological time, arriving empty and leaving to join the bank of finished moments in a past never to return: "This is the time of capitalism, colonialism, and militarism" (Barad, 2017b, p. 60). For agential realists, the present, as in Benjamin's thick-now, is haunted, and full of multiple pasts and possible futures, it is "a constellation or entangled configuration of moments" (Juelskjær et al., 2021, p. 134). In Chapter 3, Vrygrond tells the story of ongoing geopolitical hauntologies of racialised capitalism, gang violence, housing backlogs, high crime levels, fatal diseases, and migrancy that are entangled with/in traumatic geopolitical and spatial realities of living in post-Apartheid South Africa. Chapter 5 further stories with the ghostly matter of the militarism of Apartheid that engulfs the present. For example, schooling and education in South Africa are alive with temporal-spatial multiplicities of exclusion, space and land.

Co-created narrative vignettes throughout the book make visible how agential realism draws attention to the 'doings' and 'becomings' of the world rather than assuming its pre-existing and discoverable nature. Meaning made through material enactments is tied to its specific diffractive relations. In Chapter 6, the vignette involving Zuko and the plastic bricks is 'read' first through a humanist lens—assigning agency to the human child—and then diffractively, as a *phenomenon*. In a diffractive analysis, the phenomenon is open and ongoing in that all parts of the relation are agentic and are mutually co-constituting the phenomenon. The bricks complexify the relations between humans and the commodification of play involving 'cheap' labour and environmental damage. Zuko's particular use of the bricks troubles some deeply rooted humanist assumptions about Adult researcher and 'observed' child.

Knowledge is always political and implicated in the material becoming of the world. Haraway's call to action in the Anthropocene, "make kin, not babies!"[2] (Haraway, 2016, p. 102), is an expression of the inseparability of fact, fiction, fabulation, and figuration: scientific facts and ethical judgements cannot be separated or categorised as different disciplinary concerns. Scientific fact is produced not only by discursive paradigms, but those paradigms also drive material and political action and impact. Colonialism has produced 'north' and 'south' and the knowledges made possible by a Newtonian conception of time and place. However, both Latour (2004) and Haraway (2016) recognise that the powerful critique of 'pure science' made by post-structuralist deconstructions in the 1980s and 1990s is being put to work by both sides of the climate change debate. Critique may not be the most effective tool in this era, especially when it is used competitively and dismissively for its own end. Questions about climate and ecologies that are implicated in the ongoing of multi-species living and thriving on this planet demand that something more collaborative and creative be called upon. As postqualitative researchers we call upon the world (as a verb) (van Dooren & Rose, 2016) to provide this alternative. Critique is reconfigured through a *diffractive methodology*.

As Malou Juelskjær and colleagues put it strikingly: "diffraction, when enacted in agential realism, is primarily a quantum-physical phenomenon related to how the world worlds itself" (Juelskjær et al., 2021, p. 12). In other words, the diffractive methodology de(con)structs how we tend to read data. It troubles the ontology of data as independently existing bodies with precise 'edges' and boundaries separated from their 'context' and 'other' bodies. Data and texts are not mirrors, reflections, or representations of a world or a reality existing separately from the doings of the research and the researchers as 'parts' of that data. Texts are always already in relation, which also changes how we think about 'critique'.

Diffraction is a relational, feminist form of academic engagement (Murris & Bozalek, 2019b) and has profound implications for the future in a higher education environment that is more welcoming, open, collaborative, and activist.

We believe that it is imperative, when orienting new researchers into the key concepts of research, to be explicit and transparent about the Worlds these concepts presuppose and to which they commit themselves (see Chapter 3). Working with concepts also requires that we notice what is excluded or invisible in these conceptions. "Theorizing is a continual re-turning, further elaborating, interrupting, continuing to put it in conversation with other crucial insights, projects, practices" (Barad in Juelskjær et al., 2021, p. 134).

Throughout this book, we have used a diffractive methodology as a way of responding response-ably to data. This methodology—initially proposed by Haraway (1997, 1988) is itself diffracted through by various feminist philosophers and science studies scholars (Barad, 2014). Diffraction as a methodology offers affirmative readings of different kinds of texts (Barad, 2007, 2014). A diffractive reading is different from critique in that texts/theories are respectfully read through each other in a relational way, looking for creative and unexpected provocations, strengthening these, rather than using an atomistic binary logic to compare one with the other in a representationalist manner or to create maps—objective 'views from nowhere' (Murris & Bozalek, 2019a).

Since the Ancient Greeks, in Western thought, optical metaphors have been foundational in grounding representational epistemologies. As Barad (2007, p. 86) argues, representationalism makes us believe that words, concepts, ideas, and the like accurately reflect or mirror the things to which they refer and therefore that it is possible "to turn the mirror back on oneself." As Barad (2007, p. 86) comments: "[it] makes a finely polished surface of this whole affair." As our diffractive engagement with the vignettes in this book articulates, staying with the specificity of data is not about polishing, but about complexifying and opening up less familiar transdisciplinary enquiries that took us by surprise when tracing phenomena. As a quantum entanglement, "each moment is an infinite multiplicity" (Barad, 2014, p. 169). For example, when joy plays across Della's face as she draws the pearl glove in her diary and makes us wait and guess what she is drawing, the energetic flow of 'joy' cannot be confined to her 'agency' or her playful engagement with the diary. A diffractive tracing of the play event connects with a playworlding of performative spectacle (the WWE Smackdown play phenomenon), fashion, and wild shimmering earth bodies (pearls, play-fighting animals, migratory birds, and their feathers) *and us as researchers*. These worlds connect with multiple other relational worlds and perplexing questions which are always and already connected with more and 'bigger' questions about our un/becomings as earth dwellers. We are increasingly threatened by 'our' own destructive and extractive patterns of existence and haunted by the questions they raise.

The Baradian notion of quantum entanglement troubles all binaries at their very core, including – the distinction 'between' Adult and child, and digital and non-digital—particularly important for this book and for educational research. As we argued in Chapters 2 and 6, it is impossible and pointless to attempt to track the boundaries between the digital and non-digital in children's play. Similarly, it is not helpful to track the movement of flow from one to the other. The two do not exist as discrete entities nor does one precede the other. Postdigital play is a worldly phenomenon that emerges agentially through co-configurations of becoming.

We are a community of researchers who over the course of this book writing have migrated across oceans, had children, continued with doctoral studies and taken up different work placements. Digital connectivity and communication platforms have enabled our ongoing contact and co-writing (Figure 7.3). From the first picnic table at the conference in Cape Town in 2019 (Figure 1.1), to the table at Scarborough in 2020 (Figure 1.2) (a last pre-COVID-19 face-to-face meeting), to three years of online meetings and then a bodily re-turn to the 2023 research event, again in Cape Town, connections were continually created, maintained and flexibly reconfigured a number of times through Zoom, Teams, WhatsApp, and Google Docs. Frames created through our camera lenses allow intimate glimpses of daily realities and changing moods and sound notes from multispecies voices, cutlery and dishes, paper and wind. Recordings of meetings hang somewhere/nowhere as possible returnings.

FIGURE 7.3   Line drawing/Online meeting with South African CTAP research team

Staying with the specificity of the data

Durational and iterative storying with data (slowing down; staying with; re-turning; unfolding; turning over; diffracting) have us feeling our way. Haraway (2016, p. 31) notes that *tentacle* comes from the Latin *tentaculum*, meaning "feeler," and *tentare*, meaning "to feel" and "to try". The length (and layers) of time we have stayed with the CTAP project and the data—recurring and reconfiguring—have enabled a 'slow' attentiveness necessary for following threads and tracing connections (Leibowitz & Bozalek, 2018) in our deep commitments to response-able research practices. Donna Haraway argues that cultivating response-ability involves taking "the risk of being for some worlds rather than others and helping to compose those worlds with others" (Haraway, 2016, p. 178). This involves telling stories of a particular kind as we have done throughout this book, through vignettes that challenge power-producing binaries and produce different ways of understanding how concepts work such as 'agency', 'causality', 'time', and 'space' These concepts underpin developmental notions of child development (Murris, 2019).

In our preparation for the project celebration event, we decided to create a press release in the hopes that it would encourage a broader audience of researchers, educators, media, and community attendance. What we encountered was a stark reminder of what tends 'to make news'. Some of the questions we were asked about the press release were, 'Could you please add more information about the findings and what they mean for the South African context? Are our children on track? Are they not on track? Are we making progress, or are we regressing? Are there any numbers we can cite? How do children in SA fare against their counterparts in the UK?

The stating of 'hard facts' is generally well received by the media. But what makes a good story for the local press? Or, in Haraway's words, what kind of worlds will these stories compose?

Being 'on track' implies having to perform against a set of prescribed standards and universal measures predominantly set by the agendas of the north. Systems of measuring, testing, and standardising, assume that results are neutral representations of already existing realities. But they are agentially colonising moves through which child is rendered less capable. Postdevelopmental approaches push against apparatuses that measure children as lacking and 'less than'. Representational epistemologies produce descriptions and definitions framed as either 'objective' and 'universal' (in a World of Objects), or 'subjective' and 'particular' (in a World of Subjects). Neither research paradigm works with the posthumanist interpretation of 'situatedness', which we have put to work in our reading of the vignettes.

> *The ball-making takes place outside the front door of his house in between the corrugated zinc sheet-lined lanes. Henry's sticky taping hands move skilfully, directed by memories and movements of previous sack-ball-making. These hands lead the storying as he educates the researchers.*

We resist working with generalisations or abstractions (e.g., through searching for themes or codes). Agential realism asks us researchers to stay with the specificity of phenomena. But how can we explain to the local press that we can't stop thinking-with and feel the sackball and bompie with our 'tentacles', and that engaging diffractively with some of the CTAP 'big data' in detail and precision flashes up broader ethical challenges and political opportunities for child research in the global south?

How can we possibly explain to journalists that our posthumanist research methodologies have made it possible to reconfigure humanist notions of play and trouble who and what can be playful, for example, by engaging with absences and erasures in how we transcribe data? It has even drawn our attention to what is already given (unwritten and unsaid), maybe even beyond words but is still integral to *all* research practices, for example, the binaries we tend to take for granted, such as macro/micro, or human/matter.

> *Sensations of care and love permeate the home. This is a place of living-learning relationships where conventional teaching materials like pencils, worksheets and number cards fit in snugly with other furniture.*

The experimental vignettes that constitute our re-turning to the CTAP data are an invitation to readers to attune to the specificity of the storying and the complex worlds and multifaceted realities in the global south. We might not convince the local press, but we are passionately committed to—as our book title suggests—to reconfiguring practically and theoretically what counts as 'data', 'tools', 'instruments', 'research sites', 'researchers', including the roles of technology and transcribers, as well as notions of responsibility and accountability in qualitative research methodologies. A critical role that the concept of the 'postdigital' plays is in reimagining other concepts such as 'causality', 'subject', 'object', 'relationships', 'creativity' and 'agency'. The specificities of the spacetimematterings that constitute the *becomings* of research produce new relations and possibilities for making a difference in global education research. Our visual mash-up of the research celebration event draws attention to the multiple modes of intra-connection (Figures 7.1 and 7.2).

We reconfigure 'child' and 'Adult', 'data' and 'researcher', through diffractive narratives of human and more-than-human intra-action. Play and the postdigital are present in all of the stories that we tell and that story us through the chapters and more specifically in and with the intra-connecting and agential research sites of home, school, and community spaces.

Pictures taking pictures of each other. Luzia's and Zuko's spontaneous laughter reverberates and sound waves connect through this playful event. Luzia is aware that as the watching researcher she is being watched.

We have argued throughout that a postqualitative and posthumanist orientation towards research prioritises relations as ontologically 'prior'. Phenomena, not 'things', 'objects', or 'bodies' are the objective referents. World-making is a matter of "patternings, risky co-makings, speculative fabulations" (Haraway, 2016, p. 14). Stories of swimming, water, and octopus are part of ongoing multispecies world-making. As we stay with the flows of the vignettes we encounter the ways in which worlds are made through risky and generative relations. These flows enable thinking differently about what comes to matter in research. The past seeps into the present as Seekat opens the research to unbounded ontological place relations (We rework Figure 7.3 into Figure 7.4 to make visible the flows across timespacematter).

FIGURE 7.4 Online book writing: 'meeting the universe halfway'

Joanne: … *I love this book! Because it's so, telling stories and it's giving facts.*

Joanne: *Here we go. Sy is baie slim, sy het a groot brein in haar kop, en 'n mini-brein in elke arm.* [She is very clever, she has a big brain in her head and a small brain in each arm/tentacle]

Eshal: *You see?*

Notes

1 For more about the sting, see interview between Martha Kenney and Donna Haraway on page 135.

2 Relevant for our study is that Haraway's call to action has been critiqued as being childist (Mattheis, 2022, p. 512): first, by reproducing "adultist constructions of children as passive kin 'being made.'" And, secondly, by not engaging with childhood studies and children's lived experiences (Mattheis, 2022, p. 512).

REFERENCES

Allen, R. E., & Wiles, J. L. (2016). A rose by any other name: Participants choosing research pseudonyms. *Qualitative Research in Psychology, 13*(2), 149–165.

Apperley, T., Jayemanne, D., & Nansen, B. (2017). Postdigital literacies: Materiality, mobility and the aesthetics of recruitment. In B. Parry, C. Burnett, & G. Merchant (Eds.), *Literacy, media, technology: Past, present and future* (pp. 203–218). Bloomsbury Academic.

Aslanian, T. (2018). Recycling Piaget: Posthumanism and making children's knowledge matter. *Educational Philosophy and Theory, 50*(4), 417–427.

Astuto, J., & Allen, L. (2009). Home visitation and young children: An approach worth investing in? Social policy report. *Society for Research in Child Development, 23*(4), 3–22 .

Bandura, A. (2008). Toward an agentic theory of the self. In H. Marsh, R. G. Craven, & D. M. McInerey (Eds.), *Self-Processes, learning, and enabling human potential: Dynamic new approaches* (pp. 15–49). Information Age Publishing.

Barad, K. (1996). Meeting the universe halfway: Realism and social constructivism without contradiction. In L. H. Nelson & J. Nelson (Eds.), *Feminism, science, and the philosophy of science* (pp. 161–194). Springer.

Barad, K. (2007). *Meeting the universe halfway: Quantum physics and the entanglement of matter and meaning.* Duke University Press.

Barad, K. (2010). Quantum entanglements and hauntological relations of inheritance: Dis/continuities, spacetime enfoldings, and justice-to-come. *Derrida Today, 3*(2), 240–268.

Barad, K. (2011). Nature's queer performativity. *Qui Parle, 19*(2), 121–158.

Barad, K. (2012). On touching—The inhuman that therefore I am. *Differences, 23*(3), 206–223.

Barad, K. (2013). Ma(r)king time: Material entanglements and re-memberings: Cutting together-apart. In P. Carlile, D. Nicolini, A. Langley, & H. Tsoukas (Eds.), *How matter matters: Objects, artifacts, and materiality in organization studies* (pp. 16–31). Oxford University Press.

Barad, K. (2014). Diffracting diffractions: Cutting together-apart. *Parallax, 20*(3), 168–187.

Barad, K. (2017a). No small matter: Mushroom clouds, ecologies of nothingness, and strange topologies of spacetimemattering. In A. Lowenhaupt Tsing, H. A. Swanson, E. Gan, & N. Bubandt (Eds.), *Arts of living on a damaged planet: Ghosts and monsters of the Anthropocene* (pp. 103–120). University of Minnesota Press.

Barad, K. (2017b). Troubling time/s and ecologies of nothingness. *New Formations: A Journal of Culture/Theory/Politics, 92*, 56–86.

Barad, K. (2017c). What flashes up: Theological-political-scientific fragments chapter. In C. Keller & M. Rubenstein (Eds.), *Entangled worlds: Religion, science, and new materialisms* (pp.21–88). Fordham University.

Barad, K. (2019a, August 13). *After the end of the world: …[Video].* YouTube. https://www.youtube.com/watch?v=68I0y1koakA

Barad, K. (2019b). After the end of the world: Entangled nuclear colonialisms, matters of force, and the material force of justice. *Theory and Event, 22*(3), 524–550.

Barad, K., & Gandorfer, D. (2021). Political desirings: Yearnings for mattering (,) differently. *Theory & Event, 24*(1), 14–66.

Baraniuk, C. (2023, September 9). LEGO is a company haunted by its own plastic. *Wired.* https://www.wired.co.uk/article/lego-haunted-by-its-own-plastic

Barthes, R. (1972). *Mythologies* (A. Lavers, Trans.). Hill and Wang.

Bennett, J. (2010). *Vibrant matter: A political ecology of things*. Duke University Press.

Bernardo, C. (2020. October 15). The Trojan horse Massacre: 'We had stones; they had bullets'. *University of Cape Town News*. Retrieved from https://www.news.uct.ac.za/article/-2020-10-15-the-trojan -horse-massacre-we-had-stones-they-had-bullets

Bhattacharya, H. (2008). Research setting. In L. M. Given (Ed.), *The SAGE encyclopedia of qualitative research methods* (pp. 787–788). SAGE.

Biswas, T. (2022). What takes 'us' so long? The philosophical poverty of childhood studies and education. *Childhood, 29*(3), 339–354.

Blomberg, J., & Karasti, H. (2013). Reflections on 25 years of ethnography in CSCW. *Computer Supported Cooperative Work, 22*(4–6), 373–423. https://doi.org/10.1007/s10606-012-9183-1

Bozalek, V. (2021). Slow scholarship: Propositions for the extended curriculum programme. *Education As Change, 25*(21). https://doi.org /10.25159/1947-9417/9049

Bozalek, V., & Fullagar, S. (2022). Agential cut. In K. Murris (Ed.), *A glossary for doing postqualitative, new materialist and critical posthumanist research across disciplines* (pp. 30–31). Routledge.

Bozalek, V., Zembylas, M., & Tronto, J. C. (Eds.). (2021). *Posthuman and political care ethics for reconfiguring higher education pedagogies*. Routledge.

Braidotti, R. (2002). *Metamorphoses: Towards a materialist theory of becoming*. Blackwell Publishers.

Braidotti, R. (2011). *Nomadic theory: The portable Rosi Braidotti*. Columbia University Press.

Braidotti, R. (2013). *The posthuman*. John Wiley & Sons.

Braidotti, R. (2018). Affirmative ethics, posthuman subjectivity, and intimate scholarship: A conversation with Rosi Braidotti. *Decentering the Researcher in Intimate Scholarship, 31*, 179–188.

Braidotti, R. (2022). *Posthuman feminism*. Polity.

Bucholtz, M. (2000). The politics of transcription. *Journal of Pragmatics, 32*(10), 1439–1465.

Burn, A., & Richards, C. (Eds.). (2014). *Children's games in the new media age: Childlore, media and the playground*. Ashgate Publishing, Ltd.

Burnett, C., & Merchant, G. (2020). *Undoing the digital: Sociomaterialism and literacy education*. Routledge.

BusinessTech. (2021, May 29). *Here's how much money people in Cape-Town earn based on where they live and work*. Business Tech. https://businesstech.co.za/news/finance/493609/heres-how-much-money-people-in-cape-town-earn-based-on-where-they-live-and-work/

Caton, L., & Hackett, A. (2019). Head mounted, chest mounted, tripod or roaming?: The methodological potentials of a GoPro camera and ontological possibilities for doing visual research with child participants differently. In N. Kucirkova, J. Rowsell, & G. Falloon (Eds.), *The Routledge international handbook of learning with technology in early childhood* (pp. 362–376). Routledge.

CBS Evening News. (2013, December 9). South Africa's Deadly Trojan Horse [Video]. YouTube. https://www.youtube.com/watch?v=KnWu4lAKDj0

Chisango, G., & Marongwe, N. (2021). The digital divide at three disadvantaged secondary schools in Gauteng, South Africa. *Journal of Education, 82*, 149–165.

Clark, A., Robb, M., Hammersley, M., & Flewitt, R. (Eds.). (2014). Understanding research with children and young people. *Understanding research with children and young people*. The Open University.

Cohen, L., Manion, L., & Morrison, K. (2017). *Research methods in education*. Routledge.

Cole, D. R., & Bradley, J. P. N. (2016). *A pedagogy of cinema*. Sense.

Colebrook, C. (2002). *Understanding Deleuze*. Routledge.

Colebrook, C. (2020). Is there something wrong with the task of thinking? *Environmental Philosophy, 17*(1), 39–58.

Collier, D. R., & Perry, M. (2023). Imagining research together and working across divides: Arts-informed research about young people's (post) digital lives. *Qualitative Research, 23*(1), 72–91.

Collins, B. (2023). 10 best research books for qualitative and quantitative research. *Become a Writer Today.* https://becomeawritertoday.com/best-research-books/

Comaroff, J., & Comaroff, J. (2012). Theory from the South: Or, how Euro-America is evolving toward Africa. *Anthropological Forum, 22*(2), 113–131.

Cramer, F. (2015). What is 'post-digital'? In D. M. Berry & M. Dieter (Eds.), *Postdigital aesthetics: Art, computation and design* (pp. 12–26). Palgrave Macmillan. https://doi.org/10.1057/9781137437204_2.

Creswell, J. (2020). *Educational research: Planning, conducting, and evaluating quantitative and qualitative research* Pearson Higher Ed.

Crowther, J. (2021). *'Undergoing' as posthuman literacy research in an in/formal settlement primary school in South Africa* [Doctoral Dissertation, University of Cape Town].

Crutzen, P. J., & Stoermer, E. F. (2000). The "Anthropocene". *IGBP Newsletter, 41,* 17–18.

Davis, H., & Turpin, E. (2015). *Art in the Anthropocene: Encounters among aesthetics, politics, environments and epistemologies* (p. 416). Open Humanities Press.

de Freitas, E. (2016). The moving image in education research: Reassembling the body in classroom video data. *International Journal of Qualitative Studies in Education, 29*(4), 553–572.

Deleuze, G., & Guattari, F. ([1980/1987/2004] 2014). *A thousand plateaus.* Translated and a foreword by B. Massumi. Bloomsbury.

Deleuze, G., & Guattari, F. (1994). *What is philosophy?* Columbia University Press.

Derrida, J. (1994). *Spectres of Marx: The state of the debt, the work of the mourning and the new international.* Routledge.

Descartes, R. (1968). *Discourse on method and meditations.* Penguin Books.

Despret, V. (2004). The body we care for: Figures of anthropo-zoo-genesis. *Body and Society, 10*(2–3), 111–134.

Dicks, B., Mason, B., Coffey, A., & Atkinson, P. (2005). *Qualitative research and hypermedia: Ethnography for the digital age.* SAGE.

Dixon, K. (2020). Searching for mermaids: Access, capital, and the digital divide in a rural South African primary school. In E. Morrell & J. Rowsell (Eds.), *Stories from inequity to justice in literacy education* (pp. 15–33). Routledge.

Dixon, K., & Janks, H. (2019). Researching a child's embodied textual play. In J. Rowsell, G. Falloon & N. Kucirkova (Eds.), *The Routledge international handbook of learning with technology in early childhood* (pp. 88–106). Routledge .

Edwards, S. (2023). Concepts for early childhood education and care in the postdigital. *Postdigital Science and Education, 5*(3), 777–798.

Ely, M., Vinz, R., Downing, M., & Anzul, M. (1997). *On writing qualitative research: Living by words.* Falmer.

Ensor, M. (Ed.). (2012). *African childhoods: Education, development, peacebuilding, and the youngest continent.* Springer.

Filucci, S. (2019, September 20). Parents guide to WWE Friday Night Smackdown. *Common Sense Media.* https://www .commonsensemedia.org/tv-reviews/wwe-friday-night-smackdown/ user-reviews/adult.

Fleer, M. (2020). A tapestry of playworlds: A study into the reach of Lindqvist's legacy in testing times. *Mind, Culture, and Activity, 27*(1), 36–49.

Foucault, M. (1997). *Discipline and punish.* Penguin.

Foucault, M. (2002). Space, knowledge and power. In D. Faubion (Ed.), *Essential works of Foucault 1954–1984: Vol 3* (pp. 349–364). Penguin.

Fullagar, S. (2021). Re-Turning to embodied matters and movement through postqualitative inquiries. In K. Murris (Ed.), *Navigating the postqualitative, new materialist and critical posthumanist terrain across disciplines: An introductory guide* (pp. 117–134). Routledge.

García, O. (2011). From language garden to sustainable languaging: Bilingual education in a global world. *Perspectives, 34*(1), 5–9.

Gendron, M., Van Niekerk, L., & Cloete, L. (2022). The use and value of play: Perspectives from the continent of Africa – a scoping review. *Scandinavian Journal of Occupational Therapy.* https://doi.org/10 .1080/11038128.2022.2043433

Giorza, T. (2021). *Learning with damaged colonial places: Posthumanist pedagogies from a Joburg preschool.* Springer Nature.

Group Areas Act. (1966). Act 36. Parliament of South Africa.

Gupta, A., & Ferguson, J. (1997). *Anthropological locations: Boundaries and grounds of a field science.* University of California Press.

Hall, S. (Ed.). (1997). *Representation: Cultural representations and signifying practices* (Vol. 2). Sage.

Haraway, D. (1988). Situated knowledges: The science question in feminism as a site of discourse on the privilege of partial perspective. *Feminist Studies, 14*(3), 575–599.

Haraway, D. (1992). The promises of monsters: A regenerative politics for inappropriate/d Others. In L. Grossberg, C. Nelson, & P. A. Treichler (Eds.), *Cultural studies* (pp. 295–337). Routledge.

Haraway, D. (1997). *Modest_Witness@Second_Millenium. Femaleman©_Meets_OncoMouse™: Feminism and technoscience.* Routledge.

Haraway, D. (2008). Companion species, mis-recognition, and queer worlding. In N. Giffney & M. J. Hird (Eds.), *Queering the non/human* (pp. xxiii–xxxvi). Ashgate.

Haraway, D. (2010). When species meet: Staying with the trouble. *Environment and Planning D: Society and Space, 28*(1), 53. https://doi.org/10.1068/d2706wsh

Haraway, D. (2014). Jeux de ficelles avec les espèces compagnes: Rester avec le trouble. In V. Despret & R. Larrère (Eds.), *Les animaux: Deux ou trois choses que nous savons d'eux* (pp. 17–47). Hermann.

Haraway, D. (2016). *Staying with the trouble: Making kin in the Chthulucene.* Duke University Press.

Harker, C. (2005). Playing and affective time-spaces. *Children's Geographies, 3*(1), 47–62.

Harvey, L., Cooke, P., & Bishop Simeon Trust. (2021). Reimagining voice for transrational peace education through participatory arts with South African youth. *Journal of Peace Education, 18*(1), 1–26.

Harwood, D., & Collier, D. R. (2019). "Talk into my GoPro, I'm making a movie!": Using digital ethnographic methods to explore children's sociomaterial experiences in the woods. In N. Kucirkova, J. Rowsell,

& G. Falloon(Eds.), *The Routledge international handbook of learning with technology in early childhood* (pp. 49–61). Routledge.

Haynes, J., & Murris, K. (2019). Taking age out of play: Children's animistic philosophising through a PictureBook. *The Oxford Literary Review, 41*(2), 290–309.

Heavy-Gpark. (2023, July 3). *Bompies* [Video] [YouTube]. https://www.youtube.com/watch?v=rfOYMuSbh-U.

Horst, H. A., & Gaspard, L. (2020). Platforms, participation and place: Understanding young people's changing digital media worlds. In L. Green, D. Holloway, K. Stevenson, T. Leaver, & L. Haddon (Eds.), *The Routledge companion to digital media and children* (pp. 38–47). Routledge.

Hov, A. M., & Neegaard, H. (2020). The potential of chest mounted action cameras in early childhood education research. *Nordic Studies in Science Education, 16*(1), 4–17.

Hughes, B. (2002). *A playworker's taxonomy of play types* (2nd ed.). PLAYLINK.

Imoh, A. T. D. (2016). From the singular to the plural: Exploring diversities in contemporary childhoods in sub-Saharan Africa. *Childhood, 23*(3), 455–468.

Imoh, A. T. D., Tetteh, P. M., & Oduro, G. Y. (2022). Searching for the everyday in African childhoods: Introduction. *Journal of the British Academy, 10*(s2), 1–11.

Ingold, T. (2011). *Being alive: Essays on movement, knowledge and description*. Taylor & Francis.

Ingold, T. (2015). *The life of lines*. Routledge.

Ingold, T. (2018). *Anthropology: Why it matters*. Wiley.

De Poe. (n.d). Knowledge by acquaintance and knowledge by description. In *Internet Encyclopaedia of Philosophy*. Retrieved October 14, 2023, from https://iep.utm.edu/knowacq/

Jackson, A. Y., & Mazzei, L. (2011). *Thinking with theory in qualitative research: Viewing data across multiple perspectives*. Routledge.

Jandrić, P. (2023). History of the postdigital: Invitation for feedback. *Postdigital Science and Education, 5*(3), 493–508.

Jandrić, P., Knox, J., Besley, T., Ryberg, T., Suoranta, J., & Hayes, S. (2018). Postdigital science and education. *Educational Philosophy and Theory, 50*(10), 893–899.

Jandrić, P., MacKenzie, A., & Knox, J. (2022). Postdigital research: Genealogies, challenges, and future perspectives. *Postdigital Science and Education*, 1–12. https://doi.org/10.1007/s42438-022-00306-3

Jenks, C. (2005). *Childhood* (2nd ed.). Routledge.

Jewitt, C. (2012). An introduction to using video for research NCRM working paper. *NCRM* (Unpublished).

Johnson, W. J. (2018). *The feather thief: Beauty, obsession, and the natural history heist of the century.* Hutchinson.

Jones, L., & Holmes, R. (2014). Studying play through new research practices. In L. Brooker, S. Edwards, & M. Blaise (Eds.), *SAGE handbook of play and learning* (pp. 128–139). Sage.

Juelskjær, M., Plauborg, H., & Adrian, S. W. (2021). *Dialogues on agential realism: Engaging in worldings through research practice.* Routledge.

Kennedy, D. (2006). *The well of being: Childhood, subjectivity and education.* SUNY Press.

Kind, S. (2013). Lively Entanglements: The doings, movements and enactments of photography. *Global Studies of Childhood, 3*(4), 427–441.

Kleinman, A., & Barad, K. (2012). Intra-actions. *Mousse Magazine, 34*(13), 76–81.

Knoblauch, H., & Schnettler, B. (2012). Videography: Analysing video data as 'focused' ethnographic and hermeneutical exercise. *Qualitative Research, 12*(3), 334–356.

Knox, J. (2019). What does the 'postdigital' mean for education? Three critical perspectives on the digital, with implications for educational research and practice. *Postdigital Science and Education, 1*(2), 357–370.

Kohan, W. (2015). *The inventive schoolmaster.* Sense.

Koro-Ljungberg, M., Ulmer, J., & MacLure, M. (2018). D . . . a . . . t . . . a . . . , data++. data, and some problematics. In N. K. Denzin & Y. S. Lincoln (Eds.), *The SAGE handbook of qualitative research* (5th ed., pp.462–484). Sage Publications.

Kuby, C. (2021). What paradigmatic perspectives make possible: Considerations for pedagogies and the doing of inquiry. In K. Murris (Ed.), *Navigating the postqualitative, new materialist and critical posthumanist terrain across disciplines: An introductory guide* (pp. 43–62). Routledge.

Kuhn, C., Khoo, S. M., Czerniewicz, L., Lilley, W., Bute, S., Crean, A., … MacKenzie, A. (2023). Understanding digital inequality: A theoretical kaleidoscope. *Postdigital Science and Education, 5*(3), 894–932.

Lahman, M. K., Rodriguez, K. L., Moses, L., Griffin, K. M., Mendoza, B. M., & Yacoub, W. (2015). A rose by any other name is still a rose? Problematizing pseudonyms in research. *Qualitative Inquiry, 21*(5), 445–453.

Lakoff, G., & Johnson, M. (1980). *Metaphors we live by.* University of Chicago Press.

Latour, B. (2004). Why has critique run out of steam? From matters of fact to matters of concern. *Critical Inquiry, 30*(2), 225–248.

Latour, B. (2005). *Reassembling the social: An introduction to Actor-Network-Theory.* Oxford University Press.

Lazzarato, M. (2007). Machines to crystallize time: Bergson. *Theory, Culture and Society, 24*(6), 93–122.

Le Grange, L. (2018). The notion of Ubuntu and the (post)humanist condition. In J. Petrovic & R. Mitchell (Eds.), *Indigenous philosophies of education around the world* (pp. 40–60). Routledge.

Lee, L., Kurcikova, N., Rowsell, J., & Falloon, G. (2019). When technology met real-life experiences: Science curriculum project with technology for low-Income Latino preschoolers. In N. Kucirkova, J. Rowsell, & G. Falloon (Eds.), *The Routledge international handbook of learning with technology in early childhood* (pp. 338–349). Routledge.

LEGO Foundation. (2020). *Learning through play experience tool: Zooming in on the five characteristics of learning through play.* LEGO Foundation. https://cms.learningthroughplay.com/media/l2no4unb/the-learning-through-play-experience-tool-an-introduction.pdf.

Leibowitz, B., & Bozalek, V. (2018). Towards a slow scholarship of teaching and learning in the South. *Teaching in Higher Education, 23*(8), 981–994.

Lemieux, A. (2021). What does making produce? Posthuman insights into documenting relationalities in maker education for teachers. *Professional Development in Education, 47*(2–3), 493–509.

Lenz Taguchi, H. (2010). *Going beyond the theory/practice divide in early childhood education: Introducing an intra-active pedagogy.* Routledge.

Levebvre, H. (1991). *The production of space* (D. Nicholson, Trans.). Blackwell.

Lien, M., & Pálsson, G. (2021). Ethnography beyond the human: The 'other-than-human' in ethnographic work. *Ethnos, 86*(1), 1–20.

Lifehack Laboratories LLC. (2023). *20 best educational research books of all time.* Bookauthority. https://bookauthority.org/books/best -educational-research-books

Lindqvist, G. (1995). *The aesthetics of play: A didactic study of play and culture in preschools.* Gotab.

Lindqvist, G. (2003). Vygotsky's theory of creativity. *Creativity Research Journal, 15*(4), 245–251.

Livingstone, S., & Pothong, K. (2022). Imaginative play in digital environments: Designing social and creative opportunities for identity formation. *Information, Communication and Society, 25*(4), 485–501.

MacLure, M. (2013). Researching without representation? Language and materiality in post-qualitative methodology. *International Journal of Qualitative Studies in Education, 26*(6), 658–667. https://doi.org/10 .1080/09518398.2013.788755.

MacLure, M. (2016). The refrain of the a-grammatical child: Finding another language in/for qualitative research. *Cultural Studies? Critical Methodologies, 16*(2), 173–182.

MacLure, M., Holmes, R., MacRae, C., & Jones, L. (2010). Animating classroom ethnography: Overcoming video-fear. *International Journal of Qualitative Studies in Education, 23*(5), 543–556. https://doi.org/10 .1080/09518391003645370.

MacRae, C. (2022). The Red Blanket: A dance of animacy. *Global Studies of Childhood, 12*(4), 348–358.

MacRae, C., Hackett, A., Holmes, R., & Jones, L. (2018). Vibrancy, repetition and movement: Posthuman theories for reconceptualising young children in museums. *Children's Geographies, 16*(5), 503–515.

Makalela, L. (2018). "Our academics are intellectually colonised": Multi-languaging and fees must fall. *Southern African Linguistics and Applied Language Studies, 36*(1), 1–11.

Maldonado-Torres, N. (2016). *Outline of ten theses on coloniality and decoloniality.* Franz Foundation. http://caribbeanstudiesassociation.org/docs/Maldonado-Torres_Outline_Ten_Theses.

Marcus, G. (1998). Imagining the whole: Ethnography's contemporary efforts to situate itself. In G. Marucs (Ed.), *Ethnography through thick and thin* (pp. 33–56). Princeton University Press.

Marsh, J. (2017). The internet of toys: A posthuman and multimodal analysis of connected play. *Teachers College Record, 119*(12), 1–32.

Marsh, J., Murris, K., Ng'ambi, D., Parry, R., Scott, F., Bishop, J., ... Morris, A. (2020). *Children, technology and play.* The LEGO Foundation.

Marsh, J., Plowman, L., Yamada-Rice, D., Bishop, J., & Scott, F. (2016). Digital play: A new classification. *Early Years, 36*(3), 242–253.

Massey, D. (2005). *For space.* Sage.

Massumi, B. (2014). *What animals teach us about politics.* Duke University Press.

Mattheis, N. (2022). Making kin, not babies? Towards childist kinship in the "Anthropocene". *Childhood, 29*(4), 512–528.

Mazzei, L. A. (2013). A voice without organs: Interviewing in posthumanist research. *International Journal of Qualitative Studies in Education, 26*(6), 732–740.

Mazzei, L. A. (2016). Voice without a subject. *Cultural Studies? Critical Methodologies, 16*(2), 151–161.

Mazzei, L. A., & Jackson, A. Y. (2012). Complicating voice in a refusal to "let participants speak for themselves". *Qualitative Inquiry, 18*(9), 745–751.

McCreedy, J. (2021). WWE fan reception and shifting perceptions of masculinity in the Trump era. *Journal of Popular Television, 9*(2), 233–250.

Mengis, J., Nicolini, D., & Gorli, M. (2016). The video production of space: How different recording practices matter. *Organizational Research Methods, 21*(2), 288–315. https://doi.org/10.1177/1094428116669819.

Menning, S. F., Murris, K., & Wargo, J. M. (2021). Reanimating video and sound in research Practices. In K. Murris (Ed.), *Navigating the postqualitative, new materialist and critical posthumanist terrain across disciplines – An introductory guide*. Postqualitative, New materialist and critical posthumanist research (pp. 135–149). Routledge.

Menning, S., & Murris, K. (2023). Reconfiguring the use of video in qualitative research through practices of filmmaking: A cinematic performative analysis. *Qualitative Research*. 14687941231206755

Merriam, S., & Tisdell, E. (2015). *Qualitative research: A guide to design and implementation*. John Wiley & Sons.

Miller, E., & Almon, J. (2009). *Crisis in the kindergarten: Why children need to play in school*. Alliance for Childhood (NJ3a) College Park.

Mitman, G. (2019). Reflections on the Plantationocene: A conversation with Donna Haraway and Anna Tsing. *Edge Effects, 18*, 1–20.

Moss, P., & Dahberg, G. (2005). *Ethics and politics in early childhood education*. Routledge.

Murris, K. (2016). *The Posthuman child: Educational transformation through philosophy with picturebooks*. Routledge.

Murris, K. (2019). Children's development, capability approaches and postdevelopmental child: The birth to four curriculum in South Africa. *Global Studies of Childhood, 9*(1), 1–16. https://doi.org/10.1177/2043610619832894

Murris, K. (2022a). *Karen Barad as educator: Agential realism and education*. Springerbriefs.

Murris, K. (2022b). 'This is not a photograph of Zuko': How agential realism disrupts child-centred notions of agency in digital play research. *Children's Geographies, 21*(3), 547–562. https://doi.org/10.1080/14733285.2022.2098005

Murris, K., & Bozalek, V. (2019a). Diffracting diffractive readings of texts as methodology: Some propositions. *Educational Philosophy and Theory, 51*(14), 1504–1517.

Murris, K., & Bozalek, V. (2019b). Diffraction and response-able reading of texts: The relational ontologies of Barad and Deleuze. *International Journal for Qualitative Studies in Education, 32*(7), 872–886.

Murris, K., & Kohan, W. (2021). Troubling troubled school time: Posthuman multiple temporalities. *International Journal of Qualitative Studies in Education, 34*(7), 581–597.

Murris, K., & Menning, S. F. (2019). Introduction to the special issue: Videography and decolonizing childhood. *Video Journal of Education and Pedagogy, 4*(1), 1–8.

Murris, K., & Osgood, J. (2022). Risking erasure? Posthumanist research practices and figurations of (the) child. *Contemporary Issues in Early Childhood, 23*(3), 208–219.

Murris, K., & Peers, J. (2022). GoPro(blem)s and possibilities: Keeping the child human of colour in play in an interview. *Contemporary Issues in Early Childhood, 23*(3), 332–355.

Murris, K., & Reynolds, B. (Prods). (2018, September 5). *A manifesto posthuman child: De/colonising childhood through reconfiguring the human* [Video] YouTube. https://www.youtube.com/watch?v=ikN-LGhBawQ

Murris, K., & Zhao, W. (2022). Non/representational. In Murris, K. (Ed.), *A glossary for doing postqualitative, new materialist and critical posthumanist research across disciplines* (pp. 92–93). Routledge.

Murris, K., Scott, F., Stjerne Thomsen, B., Dixon, K., Giorza, T., Peers, J., & Lawrence, C. (2022). Researching digital inequalities in children's play with technology in South Africa. *Learning, Media and Technology, 48*(3), 542–555.

Nandy, A. (1987). Reconstructing childhood: A critique of the ideology of adulthood. In A. Nandy (Ed.), *Traditions, tyranny, and utopias: Essays in the politics of awareness* (pp. 41–56). Oxford University Press.

Nansen, B., Nicoll, B., & Apperley, T. (2019). Postdigitality in children's crossmedia play: A case study of Nintendo's amiibo figurines. In G. Mascheroni, & D. Holloway (Eds.), *The internet of toys: Practices, affordances and the political economy of children's smart play* (pp. 89–108). Palgrave Macmillan.

Neimanis, A. (2017). *Bodies of water: Posthuman feminist phenomenology.* Bloomsbury Academic.

Nolfo, A. P., Casetta, G., & Palagi, E. (2022). Visual communication in social play of a hierarchical carnivore species: The case of wild spotted hyenas. *Current Zoology, 68*(4), 411–422.

Nxumalo, F. (2019). *Decolonizing place in early childhood education.* Routledge.

O'Connor, J., Fotakopoulou, O., Johnston, K., Kewalramani, S., & Ludgate, S. (2023). Resisting hyperreality? Talking to young children about YouTube and YouTube Kids. *Contemporary Issues in Early Childhood.* https://doi.org/10.1177/14639491231 166487.

Osgood, J. (2019). Materialized reconfigurations of gender in early childhood: Playing seriously with LEGO. In J. Osgood, K. Robinson, & V. Pacini-Ketchabaw (Eds.), *Feminists researching gendered childhoods: Generative entanglements* (pp. 85–108). Bloomsbury.

Osgood, J., Sakr, M., & de Rijke, V. (2017). Editorial: Dark play and digital playscapes. *Contemporary Issues in Early Childhood, 18*(2), 109–113.

Oswell, D. (2013). *The agency of children: From family to global human rights.* Cambridge University Press.

Ounpraseuth, J., & Thurston, B. (2022, March 23). *Race demographics in TV wrestling viewership: AEW is still behind WWE with Black viewers.* Wrestlenomics. Retrieved from https://wrestlenomics.com /2022/03/23/race-demographics-in-tv-wrestling-Viewership-aew -is-still-behind-wwe-with-black-viewers/

Paley, V. G. (2009). *A child's work: The importance of fantasy play.* University of Chicago Press.

Parten, M. B. (1932). Social participation among preschool children. *Journal of Abnormal and Social Psychology, 27*(3), 243–269.

Patricio, M. L. (2018). *An analysis of the portrayal of WWE female performers in television and social media* [Masters Dissertation, San Francisco State University]. Scholarworks. https://scholarworks .calstate.edu/concern/theses/cc08hm244

Pedersen, H. (2010). *Animals in schools: Processes and strategies in human-animal education.* Purdue University.

Penn, H. (2005). *Unequal childhoods: Young children's lives in poor countries*. Psychology Press.

Pennycook, A. (2018) Posthumasist Applied Linguistics. *Applied Lingusitics, 38*(4), 445–461.

Percy-Smith, B., & Thomas, N. P. (Eds.). (2009). *A handbook of children and young people's participation: Perspectives from theory and practice*. Routledge.

Pettersen, K., Arnseth, H. C., & Silseth, K. (2022). Playing Minecraft: Young children's postdigital play. *Journal of Early Childhood Literacy*. https://doi.org/10.1177/14687984221118977.

PhD Assistance Editors. (2019). *What are some good books on research methodology?*. PhD Assistance. https://www.phdassistance.com/blog/what-are-some-good-books-on-research-methodology/

Point, S., & Baruch, Y. (2023). (Re) thinking transcription strategies: Current challenges and future research directions. *Scandinavian Journal of Management, 39*(2), 101272.

Potter, J., & Cowan, K. (2020). Playground as meaning-making space: Multimodal making and re-making of meaning in the (virtual) playground. *Global Studies of Childhood, 10*(3), 248–263.

Rautio, P. (2013). Children who carry stones in their pockets: On autotelic material practices in everyday life. *Children's Geographies, 11*(4), 394–408.

Rollo, T. (2018). Feral children: Settler colonialism, progress, and the figure of the child. *Settler Colonial Studies, 8*(1), 60–71.

Rose, D. B. (2017). When all you love is being trashed. In A. Tsing, H. Swanson, E. Gan, & N. Brubandt (Eds.), *Ghosts and monsters of the Anthropocene* (pp. 51–63). University of Minnesota Press.

Rose, D. B. (2021). *Shimmer: Flying fox exuberance in worlds of peril*. Edinburgh University Press.

Ross, F. C. (2005). Urban development and social contingency: A case study of urban relocation in the Western Cape, South Africa. *Africa Today, 51*(4), 18–31.

Sakr, M. (2017). *Digital technologies in early childhood art: Enabling playful experiences*. Bloomsbury Publishing.

Schrader, A. (2012). Haunted measurements: Demonic work and time in experimentation. *Differences: A Journal of Feminist Cultural Studies, 23*(3), 119–160.

Scott, F., Marsh, J., Murris, K., Ng'ambi, D., Thomsen, B. S., Bannister, C., … Lawrence, C. (2023). An ecological perspective on children's play with digital technologies in South Africa and the United Kingdom. *International Journal of Play, 12*(3), 349–374.

Shefer, T., & Bozalek, V. (2022). Wild swimming methodologies for decolonial feminist justice-to-come scholarship. *Feminist Review, 130*(1), 26–43. https://doi.org/10.1177%2F01417789211069351

Snaza, N. (2013). Bewildering education. *Journal of Curriculum and Pedagogy, 10*(1), 38–54.

Sony. (2022). *Sustainability report 2022.* https://www.sony.com/en/SonyInfo/csr/library/reports/SustainabilityReport2022_sourcing_E.pdf

St. Pierre, E. A. (2011). Post qualitative research: The critique and the coming after. In N. K. Denzin & Y. S. Lincoln (Eds.), *The SAGE handbook of qualitative research* (4th ed., pp. 611–625). Sage Publications.

Stables, A. (2008). *Childhood and the philosophy of education: An anti-Aristotelian perspective.* Continuum Studies in Educational Research.

Stevenson, K. (2021). Young children's creativity in digital possibility spaces: What might posthumanism reveal? In L. Green, D. Holloway, K. Stevenson, T. Leaver, & L. Haddon (Eds.), *The Routledge companion to digital media and children* (pp. 75–86). Routledge.

Surfer's Corner. (2022). *Muizenberg beach drone images.* Surfer's Corner. https://www.surfers-corner.co.za/

Susic, P. (2023). *PlayStation sales, numbers, revenue and users.* https://headphonesaddict.com/playstation-statistics/

Sutton-Smith, B. (1966). Piaget on play: A critique. *Psychological Review, 73*(1), 104.

Tamara, R. H., & Nugroho, B. S. (2021). Popularizing American professional wrestling as popular culture outside the United States. *Crossover, 1*(2), 1–27.

Tavin, K., Kolb, G., & Tervo, J. (2021). *Post-digital, post-internet art and education: The future is all-over.* Springer Nature.

Truman, S. (2019). Inhuman literacies and affective refusals: Thinking with Sylvia Wynter and secondary school English. *Curriculum Inquiry, 49*(1), 110–128.

Tsing, A. L. (2015). *The mushroom at the end of the world: On the possibility of life in capitalist ruins.* Princeton University Press.

United Nations. (1989, November 20). Convention on the rights of the child. General Assembly Resolution 44/25, UN Doc. A/RES/44/25. United Nations.

Vally, D. (Director). (2010). *Afrikaaps.* [Film]. Plexis Films/The Glasshouse Production.

van Beeck, L. (2020). *Learning through play experience tool: Guidelines for general use of the Learning through play experience tool.* Australian Council for Educational Research, for LEGO Foundation. https://learningthroughplay.com/learning-through-play-experience-tool.

Van Deursen, A. J., & Helsper, E. J. (2015). The third-level digital divide: Who benefits most from being online? In L. Robinson, S. R. Cotten, J. Schulz, T. M. Hale & A. Williams (Eds.), *Communication and information technologies annual* (pp. 29–52). Emerald Group Publishing Limited.

Van Dijk, J., & Hacker, K. (2003). The digital divide as a complex and dynamic phenomenon. *The Information Society, 19*(4), 315–326.

van Dooren, T., & Rose, D. (2016). Lively ethnography: Storying animist worlds. *Environmental Humanities, 8*(1), 77–94.

Van Vleet, M., & Feeney, B. C. (2015). Play behavior and playfulness in adulthood. *Social and Personality Psychology Compass, 9*(11), 630–643.

Weiser, M. (1994). The world is not a desktop. *Interactions, 1*(1), 7–8.

Whitehead, A. N. (1948). *Science and the modern world.* The New American Library.

Willemse, H. (2016). Soppangheid for Kaaps: Power, creolisation and Kaaps Afrikaans. *Multilingual Margins, 3*(2), 73–85.

Winnicott, D. (1971/2005). *Playing and reality.* Routledge Classics.

Winter, K., & Cree, V. E. (2016). Social work home visits to children and families in the UK: A Foucauldian perspective. *British Journal of Social Work, 46*(5), 1175–1190.

Wood, E. (2009). Developing a pedagogy of play. In A. Anning, J. Cullen, & M. Fleer (Eds.), *Early childhood education: Society and culture* (pp.27–38). Sage.

Wood, R., & Litherland, B. (2018). Critical feminist hope: The encounter of neoliberalism and popular feminism in WWE 24: Women's Evolution. *Feminist Media Studies, 18*(5), 905–922.

World Wrestling Entertainment. (2023, October 12). *Who we are: Company overview.* https://corporate.wwe.com/who-we-are/company-overview

Zosh, J. M., Hopkins, E. J., Jensen, H., Liu, C., Neale, D., Hirsh-Pasek, K., … Whitebread, D. (2017). *Learning through play: A review of the evidence* [White paper]. The LEGO Foundation.

INDEX

Page numbers in *italic* indicate figure and **bold** indicate table respectively

'/' *see also* agential cut; cutting together-apart; 'forward slash'